THE SUICIDE

D1242406

*Nikolai Erdman
adapted by
Richard Nelson
from a literal
translation
by Xenia Youhn*

BROADWAY PLAY PUBLISHING INC
56 E 81st St., NY NY 10028-0202
212 772-8334 fax: 212 772-8358
http://www.BroadwayPlayPubl.com

THE SUICIDE
© Copyright 2000 by Richard Nelson

First printing: June 2000
ISBN: 0-88145-173-8

Book design: Marie Donovan
Word processing: Microsoft Word for Windows
Typographic controls: Xerox Ventura Publisher 2.0 P E
Typeface: Palatino
Copy editing: Michele Travis
Printed on recycled acid-free paper and bound in the U S A

Published by Broadway Play Publishing Inc

ORIGINAL PRODUCTION

This adaptation of THE SUICIDE was commissioned and first produced by The Goodman Theater (Gregory Mosher, Artistic Director). It was first performed on 9 October 1980 with the following cast and creative contributors:

SEMYON PODSEKALNIKOV .... Seth Allen
MASHA PODSEKALNIKOV .... Audrie J Neenan
SERAFIMA .... Margaret Hilton
ALEXANDER KALABUSHKIN .... Gabor Morea
MARGARITA IVANOVNA .... Mary Cobb
ARISTARKH .... Eugene Troobnick
CLEOPATRA MAXIMOVNA .... Kate McGregor-Stewart
EGOR TIMOFEEVICH .... Jack Hallett
PUGACHEV .... Dennis Kennedy
FATHER ELPIDI .... David E Chadderdon
VIKTOR VIKTOROVICH .... Tim Halligan
RAISA FILLIPOVNA .... Annabel Armour
A DEAF AND DUMB BOY .... Lev Joffe
AN OLD WOMAN .... Diane Dorsey
A WAITER .... Mitch Webb
A SEAMSTRESS .... Diane Dorsey
MEN .... Dennis Kennedy & Mitch Webb
A DELIVERY BOY .... Lev Joffe
TWO MEN WITH A COFFIN Tim Halligan & Mitch Webb
TWO OLD WOMEN .... Diane Dorsey & Mary Cobb
OLEG LEONIDOVICH .... Mitch Webb

Director .... Gregory Mosher
Set designer .... Michael Merritt
Costume designer .... Christa Scholtz
Lighting designer .... Arden Fingerhut
Sound designer .... Michael Schweppe
Production stage manager .... Joseph Drummond

CHARACTERS

SEMYON PODSEKALNIKOV, *a man without a job*
MASHA PODSEKALNIKOV, *his wife*
SERAFIMA, *his mother-in-law*
ALEXANDER KALABUSHKIN, *a recent widower*
MARGARITA IVANOVNA, *his "friend"*
ARISTARKH DONINIKOVICH GRAND-SKUBIK, *a liberal*
CLEOPATRA MAXIMOVNA, *a woman with a beautiful face*
EGOR TIMOFEEVICH, *a mailman*
PUGACHEV, *a butcher*
FATHER ELPIDI, *a priest*
VIKTOR VIKTOROVICH, *a poet*
RAISA FILLIPOVNA, *a woman with a beautiful stomach*
A DEAF AND DUMB BOY
AN OLD WOMAN
A WAITER
A SEAMSTRESS
TWO SUSPICIOUS-LOOKING MEN
A DELIVERY BOY
TWO MEN WITH A COFFIN
FIRST OLD WOMAN
SECOND OLD WOMAN
OLEG LEONIDOVICH, *a great lover*

ACT ONE

(Room in SEMYON'*s apartment. Night)*
*(*SEMYON *and his wife,* MASHA, *asleep in a double bed.)*
SEMYON: Masha? Masha? Masha, are you asleep?
MASHA: *(Screams)* Ahhhhhhh!
SEMYON: What's wrong? What's wrong?
MASHA: What's wrong?
SEMYON: What's wrong? It's me.
MASHA: It's you?
SEMYON: It's me.
MASHA: Oh.
SEMYON: Masha, I wanted to ask you something.
There is something I wanted to ask you, Masha.
Masha? Masha, are you asleep?
MASHA: *(Screams)* Ahhhhhhh!
SEMYON: What's wrong? What's wrong?
MASHA: What's wrong?
SEMYON: What's wrong? It's me.
MASHA: It's you?
SEMYON: It's me.
MASHA: It's you?
SEMYON: Who else would it be?
MASHA: Oh.

SEMYON: Masha. I wanted to ask you something. Masha? Masha, are you asleep?

MASHA: No.

SEMYON: Good, because there's something I've wanted to ask you, Masha.

MASHA: What, Semyon?

SEMYON: Masha, I wanted to ask if there was any liver sausage left over from dinner.

MASHA: What?

SEMYON: If there was any liver sausage left over from dinner?

MASHA: Semyon, I should have learned by now to expect anything from you, but I'd have to admit I never expected this: that you'd wake up your exhausted wife in the middle of the night to start a conversation about liver sausage!!! Don't you ever think about anyone but yourself?!! All day I'm working like some kind of a horse, I'm running around like a chicken with its head cut off, until at night when at last I have a moment or two of a little peace and quiet to relax and sleep and calm my nerves, then you can't resist frazzling me!! You're going to kill me with this liver sausage!! Try to understand, Semyon, that just because you can't sleep, it doesn't mean other people can't sleep. Semyon? Semyon? Are you asleep?

SEMYON: *(Screams)* Ahhhhhhhhh!!!!!

MASHA: What's wrong? What's wrong?

SEMYON: What's wrong?

MASHA: What's wrong? It's me.

SEMYON: It's you?

MASHA: It's me.

SEMYON: Oh.

MASHA: I was saying that just because you can't sleep, it doesn't mean other people can't sleep, Semyon.

SEMYON: *I* know.

MASHA: And *I* know that Mama and I went out of our way to make your favorite meal tonight, and we gave you more than anyone else. So why didn't you eat then?!

SEMYON: And why did you and your Mama give me more than anyone else? You had your clever reasons. You wanted to show everyone: here he is, our Semyon, who even though he is out of work, we still give him the most. You were trying to use me to show off yourselves! Well, I won't be used like that! So I didn't eat.

MASHA: *(Tenderly)* I know, Semyon.

SEMYON: And I know that when it's just the two of us, alone here in our own bed, you begrudge me even the tiniest taste of liver sausage. That's what I know.

MASHA: I'd never begrudge you anything, Semyon. Here, my pigeon, I'm getting you your sausage. *(She gets out of bed. Lights a candle. Barefooted, with candle in hand, she goes to the door)* What is happening to us? No one should have to live like this. *(Goes out. Returns with a plate of sausage and bread)* White bread or black bread, my pigeon?

SEMYON: I don't care if it's blue bread, I'm not going to touch it.

MASHA: Blue bread? I don't think I've ever seen blue bread.

SEMYON: I mean—I don't care what the color of the bread is, I am not going to eat.

MASHA: No?

SEMYON: You can bold my nose and shovel it through my teeth but I won't swallow.

MASHA: But why, Semyon?

SEMYON: Because you won't just spread the liver
sausage, you'll have to preach at me first. And by
the time you've finished preaching, I'll be too worn
out from listening to your crap to eat that crap.
So why bother? Get back in bed.

MASHA: Now that you mention it, Semyon...

SEMYON: I said, get back in bed.

MASHA: Wait, Semyon...

SEMYON: Get into bed!

MASHA: I'll spread it on first and then get into bed.

SEMYON: No, you won't.

MASHA: Yes, I will.

SEMYON: Who's the husband here anyway? Me or you?
Or maybe you think because I don't have a job, I
shouldn't be listened to?! You'd be wise, Masha, to
think about what being unemployed means to me.
How it has affected me. I'm a shell. Look at this...
(Sits up, throws off the blanket, puts one leg over the other,
hits himself under the knee with the edge of his palm, then
throws his leg upward) See that?

MASHA: What is it?

SEMYON: A symptom. (Lies back down, covers himself with
the blanket)

MASHA: How are we expected to live like this? If it were
a play, at least then we could laugh.

SEMYON: So what's that supposed to mean? What do
you want me to do, croak? Is that it? Is that what you'd
like? I wouldn't be half so much trouble if I were a
corpse, would I, Masha? Well maybe you'll get your
wish. But first let me just tell you one thing, dear
Masha, here in the privacy of our own room, between
you and I, Masha—you are a bitch.

(MASHA *gasps.*)

SEMYON: A bitch! You are scum! I hate you! I hate you!

(*The candlestick falls out of her hands and breaks. Room is dark again.*)

(*Pause*)

(SERAFIMA *enters in darkness.*)

SERAFIMA: Masha, the noise. What's been going on up here? You'll wake the whole house. I hope you two didn't break your bed. Masha? Masha? Is that you? Are you crying? Semyon, what's happened? Semyon? Why are you crying, Masha? Masha? Why don't you say something, Masha?

MASHA: I have my reasons.

SERAFIMA: What kind of answer is that?

MASHA: Ask Semyon. He's got the big mouth.

SERAFIMA: Semyon! Semyon! Say something Semyon!

MASHA: He's just trying to spite me, Mama.

SERAFIMA: Semyon, are you playing a game? Semyon!

MASHA: Tell my mama what you said. Tell her.

SERAFIMA: Semyon!

MASHA: Tell her, Semyon. Semyon? Semyon! (*Gasps*)

SERAFIMA: What is it? What is it?

MASHA: Maybe he had a stroke, Mama.

SERAFIMA: A stroke! What have you two been doing up here? Did you break your bed?

MASHA: (*Steps*) Hello? Semyon? Are you there? Semyon!!! Mama!

SERAFIMA: What?

MASHA: Light the candle.

SERAFIMA: What's happened? What's happened?

MASHA: Light the candle. Quick.

SERAFIMA: Where is it? Where?

MASHA: On the floor, Mama. It's somewhere on the floor. Feel around on the floor... It's there somewhere.... Semyon, my little pigeon, you're giving me a terrible fright...Semyon! How are you doing, Mama?

SERAFIMA: I'm crawling. I'm on the floor and I'm crawling.

MASHA: Not there, Mama. Crawl over there, by the rubber plant.

(Silence, something falls.)

MASHA: What was that?

SERAFIMA: The rubber plant.

MASHA: I'm losing my mind, Mama. I'm telling you, I am losing my mind!

SERAFIMA: Don't rush into anything! I still haven't crawled along by the dresser. I found it! I found it!

MASHA: Light it. Light it.

SERAFIMA: I will. I will. *(Strikes a match)*

MASHA: I just know something awful has happened! *(Running to the bed with the candle)*

SERAFIMA: Let me see! Let me see!

MASHA: *(Pulls the covers back)* Do you see anything?

SERAFIMA: No.

MASHA: Me neither... Mama, he's not here! And his side of the bed's cold. Semyon!...Semyon!... He's gone....

SERAFIMA: Gone where?

MASHA: Just gone. *(Rushes around the room)* Semyon!... Semyon!

SERAFIMA: *(With candle, peeking into the next room)* Semyon? Hello? Semyon?

MASHA: The candle! Give me the candle! *(Grabs the candle, puts it on the floor, gets on her knees and looks under the bed)* Oh there they are. *(Crawls under the bed)*

SERAFIMA: What are you doing? What are you doing under there? Have you gone mad?

MASHA: *(From under the bed)* I'm going out, Mama. I'm going out to look for him. *(Crawls out with slippers)* I've been looking for these. Get me my skirt, Mama.

(SERAFIMA rushes to the dresser.)

MASHA: Leave the candle here. *(Rushes back, replaces the candle, rushes back to the dresser)* I'll get it myself. *(Runs to the wall, snatches a skirt from a nail)*

SERAFIMA: Where are you going to look, Masha?

MASHA: Everywhere. Anywhere. Must find him. Must. He's in such a state. He's in such a state. In bed he even showed me a symptom.

SERAFIMA: A symptom! In bed!

MASHA: Do you know what?

SERAFIMA: What?

MASHA: What if he tries to do something, Mama.

SERAFIMA: Do something????

MASHA: To himself!

SERAFIMA: Of course! Of course! Why didn't you think of that before?! Hurry! Put on your shoes. Put them on. Put them on!

MASHA: My blouse, my blouse hand it to me!

SERAFIMA: Pants!

MASHA: Pants? I don't need pants.

SERAFIMA: His pants. If his pants are here, then he's still here.

MASHA: But maybe he left without his pants; he was in such a state, Mama, such a state.

SERAFIMA: I've never known a man to be in such a state.

MASHA: Then where is he, Mama?!

SERAFIMA: Maybe he had business.

MASHA: Business? Oh, business. Then that's where he's going to do it!

SERAFIMA: Do what?

MASHA: To himself! Poop and it's all over.

SERAFIMA: Holy Mother of God!

MASHA: Mama, what are we going to do?

SERAFIMA: Quiet! what do you hear?

MASHA: Nothing. And you?

SERAFIMA: Nothing.

MASHA: This is so awful, Mama! I'll go knock on the door. What is to be, is to be.

(She leaves; SERAFIMA *turns her face to the icon and crosses herself.)*

SERAFIMA: *(To icon)* Blessed Virgin, open the door of mercy and let us in.

MASHA: *(Running in)* It's locked from the inside.

SERAFIMA: Did you speak to him?

MASHA: I spoke.

SERAFIMA: Well, how is he?

MASHA: He wouldn't answer me.

SERAFIMA: Then maybe he's no longer with us.

MASHA: No, he's with us.

SERAFIMA: How do you know?

MASHA: I could hear what he was doing.

SERAFIMA: Oh. So what do we do now Masha?

MASHA: I'll go wake up Comrade Kalabushkin, Mama. He'll break down the door.

SERAFIMA: Oh, I wouldn't do that, Masha.

MASHA: Why not?

SERAFIMA: Comrade Kalabushkin is racking his brains with grief.

MASHA: He's doing what?

SERAFIMA: He buried his wife just this past week.

MASHA: But that's perfect. Then he'll be able to sympathize with us.

SERAFIMA: But what if we make things worse for him, Masha?

MASHA: Mama, we can't worry about every little thing. We need a man. We women just can't manage by ourselves. *(Knocks on the door)* Go, Mama and listen at the door, you might hear him stirring. Go. Go.

(She leaves.)

MASHA: Comrade Kalabushkin...Comrade Kalabushkin!

ALEXANDER: *(Behind the door)* Who's there?

MASHA: It's me. I hope I'm not intruding, Comrade Kalabushkin.

ALEXANDER: Huh?

MASHA: It's me. Masha, Comrade Kalabushkin!

ALEXANDER: Who?

MASHA: Masha! Masha!

ALEXANDER: What do you want?

MASHA: I need you, Comrade Kalabushkin. I need you desperately!

ALEXANDER: How do you need me?

MASHA: As a man!

ALEXANDER: What? Did I hear you right? Not so loud.

MASHA: I know this is a difficult time for you, Comrade Kalabushkin. But I'm alone...I am completely alone. I don't know what to do.

ALEXANDER: Sponge yourself with cold water.

MASHA: What? Comrade Kalabushkin! Comrade Kalahushkin!

ALEXANDER: Not so loud! Now leave me alone.

MASHA: Then you force me, Comrade Kalabushkin, to break down the door myself!

ALEXANDER: Wait! Don't do that! Don't do that! I'm opening it! I'm opening it!

(Door flies open. In the doorway appears MARGARITA IVANOVNA—*a huge woman)*

MARGARITA: Breaking down gentlemen's doors— a peculiar pastime for a young lady. You—pardon my French—slut!

MASHA: What did I do? Condrade Kalabushkin!

MARGARITA: Shame on you. Or does the youth of today even know the meaning of the word—shame?!! I thank the good Lord I happened to be here holding Alexander's hand sharing in his deep sorrow for his beloved wife, or who knows where this shameless behavior would have led.

MASHA: What shameless behavior? I only want to break down the door.

MARGARITA: Go ahead and try, honey.

MASHA: What? Oh you don't think I meant this door? Why would I want to break down this door???

MARGARITA: Don't ask me to understand the mind of today's youth.

ALEXANDER: Margarita!

MARGARITA: What do you want?

ALEXANDER: If you're thinking of beating her up, remember: you're not registered here. *(He disappears.)*

MASHA: Beat me up? For what? What did I do?

MARGARITA: Nothing. If throwing yourself after strange men is nothing!!

MASHA: You don't think...? You don't understand, I'm married!

MARGARITA: You young women think you're so special—I'm married too!

MASHA: But he's going to shoot himself.

ALEXANDER: *(Sticking out his head)* Who's going to shoot himself?

MASHA: Semyon!

ALEXANDER: Where's he going to shoot himself?

MASHA: Well, he's going to shoot himself in the toilet.

MARGARITA: Who would ever think of shooting themselves in the toilet?

MASHA: Where else can a man without a job go?

(ALEXANDER enters.)

ALEXANDER: Then why are you just standing there? We have to do something!

MASHA: That's why I came to you. You're a military man, you manage a shooting gallery. So you can help Mama and me break down the door.

ALEXANDER: Why didn't you say this before?!

MARGARITA: What are you waiting for?

ALEXANDER: Let's go.

MASHA: Wait. If he hears us, then he'll really decide to shoot himself.

ALEXANDER: We'll sneak up on him. All at once. Very quietly. Like this. *(Takes off his slippers and tip toes)* Sh-sh! Sh-sh!

(A shout is heard.)

EVERYONE: What's that?!!

(SERAFIMA runs in)

SERAFIMA: Don't go in there! Don't go in there!

MASHA: I knew it!

ALEXANDER: What happened?

SERAFIMA: It wasn't Semyon who was in there, but Vladimir's grandmother from the other side of the house.

MASHA: Are you sure, Mama?

SERAFIMA: Of course, I'm sure. She just left. And me, like an idiot, I'm trying to look through the keyhole. She almost poked my eye out with the door knob.

ALEXANDER: An error has been made!

MASHA: And it's all your fault, Mama! I told you he was outside. Comrade Kalabushkin, hurry!

SERAFIMA: But what about his pants?

MASHA: Pants! Pants! All you can think about is his pants!

ALEXANDER: Are you sure you've looked everywhere in the house?

MASHA: Absolutely sure. We've left no stone unturned.

SERAFIMA: What about the kitchen?

MASHA: You're right, we haven't checked the kitchen. Hurry Comrade Kalabushkin. The kitchen!

(They rush to the door.)

ALEXANDER: Margarita, you stay here. The two of us can handle this.

(They leave.)

MARGARITA: What he means is they can handle each other. I don't know about you, but I'm not going to just stand out here and twiddle my thumbs...

SERAFIMA: Wait! What's that? Listen!

(From the kitchen ALEXANDER *shouts: "Stop", thunder of a slammed door, inhuman screech of* SEMYON *and finally the sound of a falling body. Silence.)*

MARGARITA: What on earth was that? Oh heavenly Mother of God!

SERAFIMA: The party's over. He shot himself. He finally shot himself.

MARGARITA: What do we do now?

SERAFIMA: I'm going to scream. That's what I'm going to do—I'm going to scream.

MARGARITA: Oh, don't!

SERAFIMA: Oh!! They're coming!

MARGARITA: They're coming?

SERAFIMA: They're carrying him!

MARGARITA: They' re carrying him? They're coming and they're carrying him?

SERAFIMA: They're coming and they're carrying him in here.

MARGARITA: In here? They're coming and they're carrying him in here?!!

SERAFIMA: What next? What next?

*(*ALEXANDER *almost drags in the terrified* SEMYON.)*

SEMYON: What happened? What happened?

ALEXANDER: Calm down, Semyon.

SEMYON: Me??? Let go! Let me go! Let me go!

SERAFIMA: Don't let him go!

MARGARITA: Hold him! Hold him!

SEMYON: Where's Masha? Masha!

ALEXANDER: Your Masha's spread out on the kitchen floor.

SEMYON: Why is she spread out on the kitchen floor?

ALEXANDER: She fainted.

SERAFIMA: What next?! What next?!

(She runs out, MARGARITA follows her.)

SEMYON: I beg your pardon, but why are you going through my pockets?

ALEXANDER: First things first.

SEMYON: What sort of things are first things? I don't even have second things. I have nothing. Do you understand me—nothing!

ALEXANDER: Don't lie to me, I saw you shove it into your mouth.

SEMYON: I shoved something into my mouth??? Will you let me up!

ALEXANDER: Alright, Semyon, I will let you up. But first give me your word that you won't do anything to yourself until you have heard me out. As a friend, Semyon, I ask only that you hear what I have to say.

SEMYON: I'm listening. I'm listening.

ALEXANDER: That's better. See how reasonable you can be when you put your mind to it. Sit, Semyon. *(Seats SEMYON. Poses)* Comrade Podsekalnikov!... Wait a minute. *(Runs to window, pulls open the curtain. The unhealthy city morning light exposes the messed up bed, the broken plant, etc.)* Comrade Podsekalnikov! Life is beautiful!

SEMYON: You can't eat beauty.

ALEXANDER: What do you mean "you can't eat beauty"? Comrade Podsekalnikov, do you know what

century this is? It is the twentieth century! It is the age
of enlightenment! The age of electricity!

SEMYON: And when they turn off the electricity because
you can't pay the bill, then—in your humble opinion,
what age is it then? The stone age?

ALEXANDER: You have a point, comrade. The stone age.
Some days it seems like that, doesn't it? Some days it's
like we are all living in caves, trapped in our little holes,
ignorant and stupid and hopeless. Some days I ask
myself, comrade, why bother? Why live? Why not just
end it all?!!... What am I saying? "Why live"??? Don't
confuse me, Semyon!! *(Poses)* Comrade Podsekalnikov!
Life is beautiful!

SEMYON: I've heard a rumor to that affect, but *Pravda*'s
already published a denial.

ALEXANDER: Your problem is that you think too much,
comrade. Follow my example, Semyon—never think!

SEMYON: A man without a job has nothing else to do.

ALEXANDER: Don't seek for answers, comrade. There
are no answers, only the struggle!

SEMYON: Don't talk to me about the struggle. Who
struggles more than me? Here, take a look at this.
(Takes a book out from under the pillow)

ALEXANDER: What's that?

SEMYON: Instructions for playing the bass tuba.

ALEXANDER: For playing the what?

SEMYON: The bass tuba. You play music on it. It's a
wind instrument. Like a trumpet, but bigger. Twenty
easy lessons is all it takes. And once mastered—here,
take a look at these figures. *(Shows him a sheet of paper)*
Let's say twenty concerts a month at five and a half
rubles a concert, that comes to thirteen-hundred and
twenty rubles a year! And that's just the beginning—

who knows what I can make once I get a reputation. You see, I've worked everything out.

ALEXANDER: I can certainly see that.

SEMYON: I've got the desire. I've got the manual. There's only one thing I haven't got.

ALEXANDER: What's that, comrade?

SEMYON: The tuba.

ALEXANDER: Ah, the tuba. There is always something, isn't there, comrade? But one learns to live with less.

SEMYON: Yes.

ALEXANDER: Yes?? Then I've convinced you? Thank you, comrade! Thank you! You've made me a very happy man! Now hand over the revolver, comrade Podsekalnikov and we'll forget this whole business.

SEMYON: What revolver? What are you talking about?

ALEXANDER: Let's not start that again. I saw you shoving it into your mouth!

SEMYON: Me? You sure it was me?

ALEXANDER: Of course I'm sure it was you.

SEMYON: Why would I shove a revolver into my mouth?

ALEXANDER: What do you take me for, an idiot? Everyone knows you want to shoot yourself.

SEMYON: Who wants to shoot himself?

ALEXANDER: You want to shoot yourself.

SEMYON: I want to shoot me?

ALEXANDER: You want to shoot you.

SEMYON: Me?

ALEXANDER: You.

SEMYON: You're sure about this?

ALEXANDER: Positive.

SEMYON: Do you know why I want to shoot myself?

ALEXANDER: Don't you know?

SEMYON: Not the specifics.

ALEXANDER: Because for the past year you've been out of work and you are ashamed at having to live off your wife. Now, tell me, isn't that a foolish reason to want to shoot yourself?

SEMYON: Very foolish. Who told you all this?

ALEXANDER: A very reliable source—your wife.

SEMYON: My wife! That bitch! Get the hell out of here! Get out! Leave me alone!!

ALEXANDER: Not until you give me the revolver.

SEMYON: What revolver? Where could I get the money to buy a revolver?

ALEXANDER: These days you don't need money, Panfidich. Down the hall would trade you one for a razor.

SEMYON: For a razor?

ALEXANDER: But you'll hand over yours for nothing. You don't have a permit. You'll get six months at hard labor. Hand over the revolver, Semyon.

SEMYON: I won't!

ALEXANDER: Then you force me to take it from you, comrade. I'm sorry, I really don't want to hurt you. *(Grabs his arm)*

SEMYON: Don't want to hurt me. Then you better get out of here, because if you don't, I'll shoot myself right in front of you.

ALEXANDER: You wouldn't.

SEMYON: Don't believe me? I'll count to three.... One!

ALEXANDER: He's going to do it!

SEMYON: Two!

ALEXANDER: I'm going. I'm going. *(Runs, out)*

SEMYON: Three! *(Pulls out liver sausage from his pocket)* What do I do with this? Where's the plate? *(Puts it on the plate)* There. Just as it was. They'll never know. Well, Masha, I'll show you.... *(Runs to the table, begins to rummage around)* I'll show you just what's it's like to live off your wife. I'll show all of you!! *(Takes out the razor)* Swedish steel. My father's. Hell with it, there'll be no more shaving for me. *(Runs out)*

(ALEXANDER enters; SERAFIMA and MARGARITA drag in the unconscious MASHA.)

SERAFIMA: What are you doing? What are you doing? Pick up her feet!

MARGARITA: Careful. Be careful.

ALEXANDER: Are you two crazy? Don't drag her along the floor! Stand her up. Stand her up!

SERAFIMA: Unbutton her clothes.

ALEXANDER: With pleasure.

MASHA: Where am I?

ALEXANDER: Among friends. So there's no need to be modest.

MASHA: Where's Semyon? Dead?

ALEXANDER: Not yet. But in five minutes? Who's to say?

MASHA: We have to find him!

ALEXANDER: I wouldn't do that. He told me himself— if you don't leave me alone, he says, I, he says, will shoot myself right in front of you, he says.

SERAFIMA: And what did you do?

ALEXANDER: This and that. I begged. I pleaded. But—no luck.

MARGARITA: At times like these, you don't get on your knees and beg, you order! Go get the police—they always know what to do in a crisis—they'll arrest him.

ALEXANDER: For what? A man can't be condemned to life. To death, yes, but not to life.

SERAFIMA: Then there's nothing we can do!

ALEXANDER: Yes there is! A tuba!

SERAFIMA: A what?

ALEXANDER: A bass tuba is our last hope for his salvation.

MASHA: What can he do with a tuba?

ALEXANDER: He can earn money. I can guarantee that if we get him this tuba, he won't shoot himself.

SERAFIMA: What does a tuba like that cost?

ALEXANDER: Maybe...five hundred rubles. Maybe a little more.

MASHA: Five hundred rubles! Tuba or no tuba, if one had five hundred rubles who'd ever want to shoot himself?!

ALEXANDER: Good point.

MARGARITA: We'll talk to my musicians. They'll pull a few strings so he can rent one.

SERAFIMA: You have musicians?

ALEXANDER: At her restaurant. You should hear them, when they play tears come to your eyes.

MARGARITA: They go under the name—A Trio of Free Artists.

SERAFIMA: For God's sake, let's speak to these artists!

MASHA: They're our last hope!

SERAFIMA: Go now and hurry!

MASHA: I'll come with you. Quick. Get ready. Quick!

(MASHA *and* MARGARITA *go into* ALEXANDER's *room.*)

SERAFIMA: I'm scared. What if you're too late?

ALEXANDER: That's where you come in. Stay here.
Distract him. Until we get back with his tuba.

SERAFIMA: Distract him how?

ALEXANDER: Use your imagination. Talk to him.
Find any pretense to talk to him and don't stop,
until we're back.

SERAFIMA: What should I talk about?

ALEXANDER: I don't know. Philosophy. Ideas.
Goodness. Happiness.But whatever you talk about
keep it light.

SERAFIMA: Keep it light?

ALEXANDER: Tell him a story. Make him laugh. Make
something up. Just don't forget that your son-in-law's
life is at stake and that's nothing to joke about. Now
get in there and talk. *(He goes into his room.)*

SERAFIMA: Let me think. How did that go...? Did you
hear the one about the Germans.... *(She goes into her
room.)*

*(SEMYON enters, Restless he looks around. Takes the revolver
out of his pocket, sits down at the table, opens the ink well,
tears off a sheet of paper.)*

SEMYON: *(Writes)* In the event of my death...

(SERAFIMA enters.)

SERAFIMA: He's not in there. *(Sees SEMYON)* Oh, God!...
Good morning, Semyon...Semyon, I will now tell you
a very distracting story. You will die laughing. Did you
hear the one about the German and the Italian?

SEMYON: No.

SERAFIMA: It seems a German was given the bird by an
Italian.

SEMYON: What Italian?

SERAFIMA: I...I don't know, Semyon. My late husband
told me this story and he just said Italian. Anyway,

this German was given the bird by this Italian who
was from somewhere either in the north or the south
of Italy. And he went home and told his father and his
father said, good, let's have it for dinner. *(Laughs. Pause)*
Let's have it for dinner. *(Laughs)*

SEMYON: So?

SERAFIMA: He gave him the bird, Semyon.

SEMYON: So?

SERAFIMA: The bird, Semyon.

SEMYON: *(Giving her the finger)* Like this?!

SERAFIMA: Yes...yes, just like that... *(He goes back to
writing.)* What do I talk about now? Ah! Oh, Semyon I
have another very distracting incident to tell you about.

SEMYON: Why don't you leave?

SERAFIMA: You will die laughing, Semyon—

SEMYON: Look, I'm very busy.

SERAFIMA: Just listen to this. There was this Turk, this
was during the war in our village, he was a prisoner,
he'd been captured, that's how he became a prisoner.
Well, anyway, he was shell-shocked. So he'd shake
his head like this...very funny. Now there wasn't very
much to do, in our village, so we got together and
thought up something to do, and that was, in the
evening, people would take bread to him. And meat-
jelly. We'd take both bread and meat-jelly and we'd
say to the Turk, we'd say, "Hungry?" and we'd show
him the bread and meat-jelly and he'd jump up and
down because he was so hungry and because he
couldn't speak Russian, but then his head would start
to shake like this, see, it looks like he's saying "No."
And so we'd wrap up the food again and say to each
other, "Guess he's not hungry," and everyone would
go home laughing. *(Laughs)* Like this. *(Laughs)*

SEMYON: Get out of here!

SERAFIMA: What's the matter? There's also the one about the coronation.

(SEMYON *jumps up, grabs pen, paper and ink.*)

SERAFIMA: Semyon, where are you going?! Stop! Semyon! About the coronation where Czarina Alexandria had a jew crushed against the palace gates!

(SEMYON *runs into the next room*)

SERAFIMA: He's not distracted. Semyon! Semyon! *(Runs after him)*

(From ALEXANDER's *room come* MASHA, MARGARITA, *and* ALEXANDER)

ALEXANDER: Let's go. We don't have much time!

MASHA: Maybe we shouldn't leave him alone.

ALEXANDER: Your mother's here, I told her how to handle him.

(They leave.)

(SEMYON *jumps out of the next room, with ink, pen and paper.*)

SEMYON: *(Shouts behind him)* One more story and I'll rip your tongue out! Back! Stay back! *(Slams the door, goes to the table, straightens the sheet of paper. Finishes writing)* In the event of my death—I blame no one. Semyon Podsekalnikov.

(Curtain)

END OF ACT ONE

ACT TWO

(Same as ACT ONE, though everything has been put back in order.)

(SEMYON sits on a stool holding a tuba. In front of him is the Teach Yourself *manual.* MASHA *and* SERAFIMA *sit to his side.)*

SEMYON: *(Reads)* "Chapter One."..."Chapter One, subtitle: how to play." "Playing your tuba is both fun and easy. Playing your tuba requires three fingers. The first finger rests on the first stop. The second finger on the second stop. And the third finger on the third stop." Like so. "Were one to blow into the tuba at this point the note B would be heard." *(Blows. Blows again)* What's wrong with this thing? A lot of air comes out, but no sound.

SERAFIMA: Masha, hold your breath. Let's hope he doesn't get discouraged.

SEMYON: Wait a second. Wait a second. Here's a chapter that deals just with blowing; it's called "How to blow". "In order to master the correct art of blowing your tuba, I—the world famous artist of sound Theodore Hugo Shultz—propose a simple and inexpensive method. Tear off a little piece of yesterday's newspaper and place it on your tongue."

SERAFIMA: On the tongue?

SEMYON: On the tongue. Come on, give me the paper!

(SERAFIMA hurriedly hands him the paper.)

SEMYON: Tear off a piece. Come on, you heard what he said.

MASHA: Smaller, smaller...

SEMYON: Now put it on.

SERAFIMA: Is it working, Semyon?

SEMYON: I-e-ae-e, o-ora-e, i-a i-e, a-e

MASHA: What?

SEMYON: U-a!!

MASHA: What?

SEMYON: U-a ya i-ai!

MASHA: I can't understand what you're saying, Semyon.

SEMYON: *(Spits out the paper)* I'm saying—you're an idiot. Understand now? Read! Keep reading! Tear off a piece of newspaper, put it on the tongue and then what?

MASHA: Then, it says, "Spit out the paper on to the floor, but keep in mind, while you are spitting, the position of your mouth. Having fixed this position of the mouth, now blow in the same way as you spit." That's all it says.

SEMYON: Now just be quiet and let me concentrate. *(Tears off another piece)* Now don't crowd me. *(Puts it on his tongue. Spits it out. Tries to blow)* What the hell! What's wrong with this thing?

SERAFIMA: The party's over. He's getting discouraged.

(SEMYON spits again, prepares to blow.)

MASHA: Dear God, if You really do exist, let there be a sound.

(Suddenly the room is filled by the tremendous roar of the tuba.)

SERAFIMA: I told you He exists. What more proof do we need!

SEMYON: Masha, go quit your job. You needn't work anymore.

MASHA: Quit my job?

SERAFIMA: But what will we live on?

SEMYON: I've worked it all out. Approximately twenty concerts a month, at five and a half rubles a concert, comes to.... Just a second. *(Searches his pockets)* I have the total here somewhere. *(Takes out a note)* Here. Comes to... "in the event of my death..." That's not it. *(Puts it away, takes out another note)* Comes to...one thousand three hundred and twenty rubles per year! And that's without even a reputation! And you ask—what will we live—

SERAFIMA: But Semyon, you haven't learned to play yet.

SEMYON: For someone like me—playing is as easy as spitting. *(Takes a piece of paper, spits, blows, tuba roars)* Hear that? That is the sound of the good life. I can just see it: I come home after a successful concert, lounge back on my sofa, surrounded by my delightful family. "Masha, have the floor polishers been by today?" "Oh yes, Semyon." "And that statue you fancied, you bought it of course." "Of course, Semyon. I bought it because I fancied it." "Very good, one needs to indulge oneself. Masha, some eggnog, please." Eggnog. That will become my daily drink. Because it's good for the lungs, and second, because I like it.

MASHA: But eggs are very expensive, Semyon.

SEMYON: Not for a man who makes... *(Looks at the paper)* ...thirteen-hundred-twenty rubles a year. And why do you care? I'm the one who's supporting us now!

SERAFIMA: The only problem is...

SEMYON: Do you mind not interrupting my practicing? If you're quiet and quit pestering me I'll let you stay and listen to music being made. *(Blows)* From now on I ask only for relative quiet during these moments of creativity. *(Reads)* "The scales. The scale is the umbilical cord of music. Having mastered the umbilical cord you are born as a musician." There's no stopping me now!!! "In order to correctly master the scale, I—the world famous artist of sound, Theodore Hugo Schultz— propose the simplest and least expensive method. Buy a cheap pia... *(Turns the page)* ...no." Why a piano?

MASHA & SERAFIMA: Why a piano??

SEMYON: Wait a minute. I must have read it wrong. "propose the simplest and least expensive method. Buy a cheap pia... *(Sees if the pages are stuck together)* ...no" Why a piano? *(Reads)* "In the appendix it is shown how to play a scale. Learn to play on the piano and then copy it on the tuba." I don't understand. A piano??? But it's not fair. A piano? Crook! He calls himself an artist of sound. Bastard! Thief! You and your umbilical cord! *(Tears the manual into pieces)* Masha! Masha? We don't have the money to buy a piano! Why did he do this to me: This was my last hope. My future was in this tuba!!!

SERAFIMA: It's not the end of the world, Semyon.

SEMYON: It is for me. How are we going to live?!

MASHA: Don't worry yourself, Semyon. We'll live like we have, off of what I make.

SERAFIMA: We've gotten by so far on what Masha earns, Semyon.

SEMYON: So I've been living off my wife, have I? So I've been a mooch? Been taking food out of your mouths! Well, I wasn't always out of a job! I did my part! Who bought these cups? I bought them. And these saucers? I did. And if these saucers break will you have enough to buy some new ones?

MASHA: We have enough.

SEMYON: Enough? Without me working?

MASHA: We have enough.

SEMYON: *(Throws the saucers down, they break)* Well, let's see then. And when these cups break will you have enough to buy new ones?

MASHA: Not enough, Semyon! Not enough!

SEMYON: There. You see now that we can't go on living like this. I know what I have to do.... Get out of here. I said—get out! You don't make enough to feed three.

MASHA: Please, Semyon, we'll manage. The three of us will.

SEMYON: How can we manage when you can't even manage to buy new cups?!

MASHA: We'll manage, Semyon, we'll manage!

SEMYON: We will, will we? *(Breaks cups)* Let's see about that. How about this vase, can you manage to buy a new vase?

SERAFIMA: Tell him, we can't manage.

MASHA: We can't manage, Semyon.

SEMYON: Ah! So you can't manage. I'm glad you've come to your senses. Now both of you, get out of here!

MASHA: You'll have to kill me first! I won't leave you!

SEMYON: You won't leave me?

MASHA: I won't leave you.

SEMYON: Let's see about that. *(Breaks the vase)*

MASHA: Semyon, you'll break everything we have!

SEMYON: You're right.

MASHA: Let's see about that! *(She breaks the mirror)*

SEMYON: You...you have the nerve...in front of my face...me, the head of this family...what's happening?!! For God 's sake leave me alone!!!! Please. Leave me alone!

(MASHA *and* SERAFIMA *go into another room.* SEMYON
locks the door behind them.)

SEMYON: Everything's smashed...the cups...the saucers...
life...the human race. All life is smashed and there's no
one left to shed a tear. The world! The Universe!...
Humanity!!! Life's just a long drawn out funeral.
(Approaches the table) What the hell, we've got by like
this up until now. *(Opens the drawer)* We'll get by. *(Takes
a note out of his pocket. Puts it on the table)* No we won't.
We won't. *(Jumps up)* I'm sorry, but I can't live like this.

*(Places the revolver against his temple. Closes his eyes.
Suddenly, a thunderous knocking on the door.* SEMYON
hides the revolver behind his back.)

SEMYON: Who is it? Who's there?

(The door opens and ARISTARKH *enters the room)*

ARISTARKH: Excuse me. Am I interrupting? I can wait
until you're finished with what you're doing.

SEMYON: Oh it was nothing. It can wait. Is there
something I can do for you?

ARISTARKH: There may be. Though first I need to know
with whom I have the honor of speaking?

SEMYON: With whom you have...? Oh you mean me!
I'm Podsekalnikov.

ARISTARKH: *The* Podsekalnikov?

SEMYON: Well, sure. Why not?

ARISTARKH: *The* Podsekalnikov who is going to shoot
himself?

SEMYON: Who told you that? Oh you mean *that*
Podsekalnikov. When you said *the* Podsekalnikov you
meant *that* Podsekalnikov. The one you probably want
to arrest for having a gun. Not me. I'm just *a*
Podsekalnikov. Just one of many.

ARISTARKH: You're not the one? But I have the address right here... *(Notices the notes)* What's this? *(Takes the note)* "In the event of my death, I blame no one, signed: Podsekalnikov". Did you write this?

SEMYON: *(Nods)* Here comes six months hard labor.

ARISTARKH: All I can say, comrade, is don't do it. You are making a terrible mistake. To shoot yourself, well; that I can understand, that's splendid, it's wonderful, go ahead and shoot yourself, but to blame no one? What a waste. Where is your social conscience? At such an important point in your life as death, one must not forget one's duty. Look around you. Look at the liberal cause, for example. What do you see? Many things. What do you hear? Nothing. And why do you hear nothing? Because it is silent. And why is it silent? Because no one dares to speak. But there is one type of man who will dare, one sort of man who will speak out, and that man comrade Podsekalnikov, is a dead man. In these times, comrade, what the living man thinks only the dead man can say. So I come to you in the name of all Russian liberals!

SEMYON: Nice to meet you. sit down.

ARISTARKH: You wish to say, farewell to life, Comrade Podsekalnikov, and with that I can sympathize. Who can live in these times? But why not blame someone? What do you have to loose? What I dare not even whisper, you can shout. I envy you, comrade. Now tell me honestly—sing it out—who do you blame?!

SEMYON: Me?

ARISTARKH: Yes.

SEMYON: Theodore Hugo Shultz.

ARISTARKH: Probably someone from the Komintern. And no doubt he is to be blamed. But he is not alone, comrade Podsekalnikov. Why single out the small fish when you can go after the whales?! Accuse them all!

I'm beginning to worry that you don't quite as yet understand why you are going to shoot yourself. Allow me to explain it to you.

SEMYON: I'd be interested. Please.

ARISTARKH: You wish to die—for the Truth! Because the Truth is what is dying! Tear up this note and write another. Get back at them. Defend us. Defend the great liberal cause and dare to ask the government the question that the government dares not to have asked: why in the area of new construction did the powers-that-be not engage the services of such a sensitive, loyal and knowledgeable man as the incomparable Aristarkh Dominikovich Grand-Skubik?!! Ask them that, and see what they say. I'd be curious.

SEMYON: Aristarkh who?

ARISTARKH: Aristarkh Dominikovich Grand-Skubik. With a hyphen.

SEMYON: Who's he?

ARISTARKH: That's me. And when, after writing such a note, you shoot yourself, you shall be a hero. The shot heard 'round Russia, a signal for a new society, and the sleeping conscience of our country will awake and speak your name. Your death shall be a rich theme for debates. Your picture paraded across the front pages of papers!

SEMYON: Tell me more.

ARISTARKH: Every Russian liberal worthy of the name will wind his way to your coffin. The best minds of the country shall be your pallbearers. Beautiful horses covered in white blankets will carry you to the cemetery, where you will be buried under wreaths, drowned in flowers.

SEMYON: Sounds like the good life, all right.

ARISTARKH: Of course I would shoot myself. But unfortunately I can't. Out of principle, you understand. *(Looks at his watch)* So it's settled. You write a rough draft of your suicide note...or maybe it'd be better if I wrote the whole thing, and then all you had to do was sign it and shoot yourself.

SEMYON: No, don't go to any trouble. I'll do it.

ARISTARKH: Bless you, comrade. You are our savior! Allow me to press you to my bosom in the name of the liberal cause! *(Embraces him)* Look at me. Not a tear when my own mother died. But look at me now. ...Look at me now. *(Leaves sobbing)*

SEMYON: I will suffer. I will suffer for everyone. And for the beautiful white horses in white blankets. Suffering—that's something I don't need a paino for. Where's some paper *(Searches)* I will bring them out of the wilderness. *(Searches)* I'll get back at them. Tremble! Tremble! Because I dare write the Truth! I'll show them no mercy! They'll read the Truth and get so sick they'll throw up. For Christ's sake. Typical. I've got the truth but no paper to write the Truth. *(Goes to the door, opens it)* I'm going out.

MASHA: Where are you going?

SEMYON: To get some paper. For the Truth. Business stationary. Give me my hat and a rouble. By the way, Masha, I've wanted to tell you that I think you should take a little more care with the way you look. I might have visitors. Some of the best minds in the country could drop by at any time.

MASHA: What's wrong with the way I look?

SEMYON: Look at your hair. Wash it. Put on a brooch And never for one second forget that you are Podsekalnikov, and that stands for...something.

(SERAFIMA with his hat and a ruble)

SERAFIMA: Some lady to see you, Semyon.

SEMYON: A lady? Let her in. Now both of you—
get in the kitchen.

(They go, CLEOPATRA MAXIMOVNA *enters.)*

CLEOPATRA: Monsieur Podsekalnikov??

SEMYON: Oui. That's me. I'm him. No question about it.

CLEOPATRA: Let us get to know each other. *(Stretches out
her hand)* Cleopatra Maximovna, but please call me
Kapochka.

SEMYON: Kapochka. Sure, I'll call you Kapochka.

CLEOPATRA: Now that we are friends, Monsieur
Podsekalnikov, I need to ask a small favor.

SEMYON: Ask. By all means, ask.

CLEOPATRA: Monsieur Podsekalnikov...may I call you
Semyon?

SEMYON: Please. Please.

CLEOPATRA: Semyon, as you are going to shoot yourself
anyway, would you be so sweet as to shoot yourself
over me?

SEMYON: Over you? You mean on top of you?

CLEOPATRA: I mean, because of me, Semyon. Shoot
yourself, because of your Kapochka.

SEMYON: Ah! Unfortunately I can't. My death's already
been spoken for.

CLEOPATRA: By Whom? By Raisa Filipovna?! How
could you, Semyon. Why? If you shoot yourself because
of that tramp, Oleg will leave me. If you shoot yourself
because of me, Oleg will leave her! Don't you see how
important this is?! Oleg is a man of refined tastes,
Raisa is a bitch, she doesn't deserve the right to touch
his feet. I tell you this because you are a sensitive man,
Semyon—you must be or why would you be shooting
yourself. Raisa chews glasses out of passion. She wants
her body kissed. Her body! She wants to kiss his body.

Body, body, body, that's how deep her mind is.
Whereas I only want to adore his soul. Only the soul,
Semyon. The soul, the soul, the soul. Defend the soul,
Semyon,and shoot yourself because of me, for the sake
of love! For the sake of true romance! And hundreds
of young girls will wind their way to your coffin and
hundreds of young men will carry you on their tender
shoulders, and beautiful women....

SEMYON: In white horse blankets?

CLEOPATRA: What?

SEMYON: I'm sorry. I got carried away.

CLEOPATRA: No, no, no, don't kiss me! Please!

SEMYON: But I'm not.

CLEOPATRA: I understand how difficult it must be,
Semyon, but you must control yourself, you must
control your urge and forget Raisa Filipovna!

SEMYON: I've never met her.

CLEOPATRA: No? Give her time. She'll be here to show
you her stomach. And she'll tell you how everyone is
crazy for her stomach. But don't be fooled, Semyon,
she tells everyone that. It's just an ordinary stomach,
I can assure you. And in any case, what's a stomach
when compared to a face? Look, monsieur!

SEMYON: I'm looking.

CLEOPATRA: Tell me what you see. Do you not see a
very beautiful face? Semyon, at home over my bed
hangs a photograph. One glance and you will loose
your mind, one look and you will cry out: "Kapochka
you have a beautiful face..."

SEMYON: Over your bed?

CLEOPATRA: Come, I'll show it to you and I swear
you won't be able to control yourself. Come with me,
and over a cup of coffee you can write.

SEMYON: Write? What do you want me to write?

CLEOPATRA: Everything you feel. How I crushed you with my charm, how I tossed you aside. How, alas, now there is no hope but death. Plumb the depths of your soul, use your imagination. You are a sensitive man, Semyon, so write something sensitive. Let's go.

(MASHA *enters, carrying in a basin of water, soap, and a sponge*)

CLEOPATRA: Come, we'd have to leave anyway—they're going to wash the floor.

MASHA: Not the floor—my hair.

CLEOPATRA: I wasn't talking to you, darling. Who is this vulgar woman?

SEMYON: She's...she's....

(MASHA *goes into the adjoining room*)

SEMYON: ...my cook.

(SERAFIMA *enters with a broom and dustpan.*)

SERAFIMA: Where are you going? Don't you want to ask the lady to stay for tea?

SEMYON: Christ! Will you just clean up this room; I'm going out for coffee with this lady.... This is...Mama...the cook's Mama. We better leave now.

(*They leave.* SERAFIMA *sweeps the floor.* EGOR *enters the room. He tiptoes toward the door and peeks through the key hole.*)

SERAFIMA: You dirty young man. Can't a woman wash herself without being peeped at?

EGOR: I peep, Serafima Ilyinishna, from a Marxist point of view and from this point of view it is impossible to have dirty thoughts.

SERAFIMA: So this point of view makes you see things differently, does it?

EGOR: Not just differently, but opposite. I proved this to myself many times. I'm walking down the street and I pass some girl. Obviously, I check her out. Her looks. Her figure. In my mind I undress her. I imagine her in bed. And I start to sweat. Then I stop myself and say— Egor now look at her from a Marxist point of view and...just like that, as if by magic, the girl turns into filth. And it works not just on women. From the Marxist point of view I can turn anything I look at into filth. I'll show you. I'll look at you.

SERAFIMA: Don't!

EGOR: I'm looking!

SERAFIMA: Help!

(MASHA enters.)

MASHA: What's happening?

SERAFIMA: Egor's looking at me!

MASHA: What are you talking about, Mama? Why shouldn't he look at you?

EGOR: See—I'm not sweating. Good morning, Masha.

MASHA: You here on business, Egor, or just passing by?

EGOR: I came about a comma, Masha Podselkanikov.

MASHA: A comma?

EGOR: I have become a writer. I've already composed one article for the paper; it's all finished except for the commas—I don't know where they go.

MASHA: Congratulations! So when is the wedding, Egor?

EGOR: What wedding?

MASHA: To become a writer you have to fall in love, because it's only through love that you can find inspiration.

EGOR: I admit, I have been inspired.

MASHA: So who is she? What's her name? Do I know her?

EGOR: Who's my inspiration?

MASHA: Yes, yes.

EGOR: Alexander Retrovich Kalabushkin.

SERAFIMA: Alexander? Are you crazy?

EGOR: Crazed I may be. It was never my intention to be a writer, but once I saw him, I couldn't control my hand, it just grabbed a pen and wrote, wrote, wrote. He's what inspires me all right.

SERAFIMA: What is it about him that inspires you, Egor?

EGOR: His carnal passion. That's what this article's about.

MASHA: His what?

EGOR: It's all here. I'll read it to you, if you tell me where the commas go. *(Reads)* "To the comrade editor of our newspaper from the mailman of the Soviet State. The scientists have proved that there are spots on the sun. And such a spot in the area of sex is Alexander Petrovich Kalabushkin, who is in charge of the scales, the 'test-your-strength' booth and the shooting gallery in the Summer Fair Garden. The 'test-your-strength' booth is not important to mailmen because we have already tested our strength in the civil war for the freedom of all laboring masses, but the shooting gallery is a different matter altogether. It is closed and has remained closed all summer. It is closed in spite of the well known desire of mailmen to want to shoot. And why does it remain closed? Because Alexander Petrovich Kalabushkin is too busy sitting like an arrogant male in a restaurant with a well known slut, Margarita Ivanovna Peresvetova. Let the editor with his iron hand take the necessary measures." Signed: "Thirty five thousand mailmen".

MASHA: Thirty-five thousand mailmen?

EGOR: My pen name.

SERAFIMA: Have you completely lost your mind?
You could get a man in trouble with a letter like that!

(ALEXANDER *and* MARGARITA *run into the room.*)

MASHA: Mr Petrovich, you're just in time. Please,
talk to Egor.

ALEXANDER: Certainly. What's the problem, Egor?

EGOR: The problem? Here's the problem: "Too busy
sitting like an arrogant male in a restaurant with a well
known slut." Where do you think the comma should
go?

ALEXANDER: Before "like".

EGOR: Before "like". Merci. I am off to the editorial
department. *(Runs off)*

MASHA: Don't you know what you've done?!

ALEXANDER: You don't think there should be a comma
before "like"?

MASHA: Don't you know who the arrogant male is?!

ALEXANDER: No, who?

MASHA: You!

ALEXANDER: Me?

MARGARITA: You!! And what slut have you been sitting
with?

ALEXANDER: Only you, Margarita.

MASHA: That's just what his letter's about: you,
the shooting gallery and Margarita.

ALEXANDER: Stop him! Bring him back! I'll open
the shooting gallery! Run! Run!

(MASHA *and* SERAFIMA *run out,* ALEXANDER *and*
MARGARITA *go into his room.*)

(NIKIFOR ARSENTYEVICH PUGACHEV, *a butcher, enters.*)

PUGACHEV: Where is everyone? No one's here.

(VIKTOR VIKTOROVICH, *a writer, enters.*)

VIKTOR: Comrade Podsekalnikov?

PUGACHEV: No. I'm waiting for him myself.

VIKTOR: Oh. I see.

(FATHER ELPIDI, *a priest, enters.*)

ELPIDI: Excuse my barging in. Podsekalnikov?

VIKTOR: No. Not me.

ELPIDI: Then you are Podsekalnikov.

PUGACHEV: No. Wrong again.

(ARISTARKH *enters.*)

ELPIDI: This must be him. Podsekalnikov?

ARISTARKH: Who? Me? No. No.

(ALEXANDER *comes out of his room, everyone rushes toward him.*)

ARISTARKH: Alexander!

PUGACHEV: Comrade Kalabushkin!

(RAISA FILIPOVNA *flies into the room like a whirlwind.*)

RAISA: So there you are, comrade Kalabushkin!
Give me back my fifteen rubles!

ALEXANDER: Sh-sh, Raisa Filipovna. Not in front of
all these people. Where are your manners?

RAISA: You tricked me: I give you fifteen rubles so
this Podsekalnikov of yours will shoot himself because
of me! So where's this Podsekalnikov now? With
Cleopatra Maximovna, that's where.

VIKTOR: Who's Cleopatra Maximovna? Alexander,
what about your promise to me?

ELPIDI: To you? But he promised me.

ALEXANDER: Comrades, comrades, comrades! When I take your money at fly shooting gallery, do I guarantee you a prize? Of course not. All I've sold you is a chance to play. And as with any chance there are risks. Our much lamented deceased is for the time being still alive so there is still hope for all of you of winning. Here, I have with me a number of potential suicide notes— *(Reads:)* "I die the victim of Zionism." "I blame no one—only the system." "Life has become unbearable with no thanks to the tax collector." And so on and so on. At the appropriate moment, he will be handed these notes, but which he will choose—is anybody's guess.

ARISTARKH: I'm sorry to disappoint you, comrades, but the decision has already been made. He is shooting himself for the sake of the liberal cause. We've had a private chat.

ALEXANDER: You shouldn't have done that, Aristarkh. I thought it was agreed that everyone would go through me.

ARISTARKH: Your clients will have to wait for the next suicide, because this one is mine.

ALEXANDER: You're the one who's going to wait.

ARISTARKH: The Russian Liberal Cause is through waiting!

PUGACHEV: So are the business men!

VIKTOR: And the artists!

ELPIDI: And the church!

ARISTARKH: Of course, we're all tired of waiting, but don't forget what the liberal cause has been through! We've been the white female slave in the harem of the proletariat!

PUGACHEV: We've been the black female slave in the harem of the proletariat!

VIKTOR: We've been the red female slave in the harem of the proletariat!

PUGACHEV: All you can talk about is art, art, art! Well, business *is* an art!

VIKTOR: All you can talk about is business, business, business! Well art *is* a business!

ARISTARKH: We will be listened to! Even if we don't have much to say.

ELPIDI: The church must win over the youth!

ARISTARKH: Yes, but how do you win over the youth of today?

VIKTOR: With ideas!

ARISTARKH: Remember how it used to be—people would have ideas which they were willing to die for. Now-a-days, people who what to die don't have ideas, and people with ideas don't want to die. There's never been a greater need for dead ideologists.

ELPIDI: Well, this dead man will be the spark that ignites us!

PUGACHEV: He'll be the flame that guides us!

VIKTOR: He'll be the fire that blazes for us!

ALEXANDER: Quiet, quiet comrades! Look why don't you just share him?

RAISA: One dead man for all of us?

PUGACHEV: Will there be enough of him to go around?

ELPIDI: It is not the body that counts, it's what lives on, on, on.

PUGACHEV: Nothing lives on, on, on. When you die you're dead.

VIKTOR: No—there is one thing that does not die.

PUGACHEV: And what's that?

VIKTOR: A little worm. Out of rotting flesh comes the worm. An eternally industrious little worm which crawls and gnaws.

PUGACHEV: And what does this little worm gnaw?

VIKTOR: He begins with the weak. Does anyone happen to know Fedia Pitunin?

ARISTARKH: No, who's he?

VIKTOR: A most remarkable character. A real go-getter. However, he is subject to moods of deep sadness. Let just one little worm get a hold of him and...well, we all know how fast worms multiply.

RAISA: What's all this about worms? He's making me sick.

PUGACHEV: He's a writer. They're paid to make people sick.

(SEMYON *enters.*)

SEMYON: You've come to see me?

ARISTARKH: They have all learned of your wonderful decision, comrade Podsekalnikov, and have come to express their delight.

PUGACHEV: You are our last hope, Podsekalnikov.

ELPIDI: A saint!

VIKTOR: A hero!

RAISA: You're my very favorite contemporary hero.

SEMYON: I wouldn't go so for as to...

RAISA: Don't be modest.

ARISTARKH: Have you decided when to shoot yourself, Podsekalnikov?

SEMYON: When? I can't say that I have.

RAISA: So modest.

ARISTARKH: Then why don't we say tomorrow at noon. That is, if it's convenient for you.

SEMYON: Tomorrow?

ARISTARKH: I mean, if it's not too long to wait.

ELPIDI: We can arrange a farewell party.

PUGACHEV: A banquet!

ARISTARKH: At say—ten o'clock tomorrow?

SEMYON: Tomorrow at ten?

ARISTARKH: For the banquet.

SEMYON: Oh, for the banquet... Yes, I think I can make it at ten.

ARISTARKH: So it's tomorrow at ten for the party and at precisely noon you can start on your journey.

SEMYON: My journey? To where?

ARISTARKH: That—is always difficult to say. Into nowhere. Into...the unknown. We'll be waiting.

SEMYON: But I don't know the way.

ARISTARKH: We'll pick you up. Don't worry.

(They leave.)

SEMYON: Don't worry. Don't worry. That's easy for you to say. I better get things in order. One cigarette case—I'll send it to my brother...in Yeletz. One coat...also to my brother...one topcoat...one pair of striped pants...no, the pants, I think, I should wear tomorrow...stripes are quite fashionable for...a banquet.

(SERAFIMA and MASHA enter.)

MASHA: Oh, I'm out of breath. We just barely caught up with Egor.

SEMYON: Here—press these pants and mend the hole. I'm going to wear them tomorrow.

SERAFIMA: Tomorrow? These are your best pants. You want to wear them out? Where are you going in them?

SEMYON: To...I...I'm getting a job.

MASHA: A job! You got a job!

SEMYON: I begin tomorrow precisely at noon.

MASHA: Finally! He got a job! What kind of job?
Temporary?

SEMYON: No, it looks pretty permanent.

MASHA: Mama, get the iron ready, we'll press them
right now!

(They run out with the pants.)

SEMYON: Tomorrow, precisely at noon. Where will I be
or what will I be at say tomorrow at half past twelve?
Or even at five after twelve? Who knows? Who?

*(OLD WOMAN and YOUNG MAN enter. The YOUNG MAN
carries a small trunk and bundle.)*

OLD WOMAN: Is it alright if he sits here.

SEMYON: Who is he?

OLD WOMAN: Anisia's nephew from the provinces.
Her door's locked so I have to go out and get the key
from her. He won't be any trouble. He's very quiet.

SEMYON: He can stay.

(She leaves. YOUNG MAN sits down.)

SEMYON: *(After a pause)* So what do you think, young
man? And for God's sake don't interrupt me until
you've thought about what you want to say. Here,
imagine that it's tomorrow. Let's say noon tomorrow
and you've just picked up a revolver. Any revolver. For
God's sake don't interrupt me. All right. Let us suppose
that you take this revolver and you now insert the
barrel into your mouth. You are inserting it into your
mouth. Good. You are inserting it. You insert. You have
inserted. And once you have inserted the barrel of this
revolver a second tics by. Now let us philosophically
examine the nature of a second. What is a second?
tic-tock. Yes, tic-tock. And between the tic and the tock

stands a wall. Yes, a wall; or in this case, the barrel of
a revolver. Do you understand? Here is the barrel.
Here is the tic. Here's the tock. And tic, young man,
is everything and tock, young man, is nothing. Nothing.
Do you understand? Now why is this? Because there is
a trigger. Let us approach the trigger philosophically.
Let's approach it. We've approached it. You press
the trigger and then you hear pif-paf. So pif is still in
the world of tic, but paf is in the world of tock. And
everything that has to do with tic and pif, I can imagine,
but everything that has to do with tock and paf, I can't.
Tik—and here I am still with myself, with wife, with
my mother-in-law, with sun and air and water —this
I can imagine. However, with tock—and here I am
without a wife—though not to have a wife is something
I could imagine—here I am without a mother-in-law—
but that too is something I could very easily imagine—
but here I am without myself, now that is something
I can't imagine at all. How can I be without myself?
What does the word "I" mean? Or the word "me"?
Me, Podsekalnikov? I am a M-A-N. Now what does
philosophy tell us about M-A-N? Darwin proved with
statistics that a man was a cell. Man is a cell. His soul
pines in this cell. That makes sense. You shoot, break
the cell and then the soul flies out. It flies out. It flies.
And as it flies out, it of course shouts: "Hosanna!
Hosanna!" And of course God beckons the soul and
He asks: Whose soul are you? Podsekalnikov's? Did
you suffer? Yes, I suffered. Well, go and dance. And the
soul begins to dance and sing. *(Sings:)* "Glory be to
God Almighty, peace on earth good will toward men."
This, I can understand. But then what? What happens
next? What do you think? Is there life after death?
(Shakes him) Look, I'm asking you, "Is there or isn't
there?" Yes or no!!! Answer me! Answer me!!

(OLD WOMAN enters.)

OLD WOMAN: I got the key. Thank you Semyon. *(Nods to the young man)* Deaf and dumb, can't say a thing.

(They leave.)

SEMYON: So tomorrow at noon. Tic...

(Curtain)

END OF ACT TWO

ACT THREE

(An outdoor restaurant in the summer fair garden.
At the table are: ALEXANDER, ARISTARKH, PUGACHEV,
VIKTOR, ELPIDI, MARGARITA, CLEOPATRA, RAISA.*)*

(SEMYON is entangled in paper streamers and sprinkled
confetti.)

(SEMYON is drinking a large glass of wine. Everyone
watches. He finishes and smashes the wine glass. Everyone
cheers and applauds.)

PUGACHEV: He acts like there's no tomorrow.

MARGARITA: That's why I love him. He's so
wonderfully wild!

(WAITER comes by.)

MARGARITA: Bill them for the glass. Drink! Drink!

SEMYON: Does anyone have the time?

MARGARITA: Twelve is still a long way off, Semyon.

SEMYON: A long way off?

MARGARITA: A long way off, Semyon. Don't think,
drink!

ELPIDI: So Pushkin goes to this Turkish bath...

SEMYON: Waiter!

WAITER: Can I help you, sir?

SEMYON: The time! What's the time?

WAITER: I imagine that it's nearly noon, sir.

SEMYON: Nearly noon?

WAITER: Nearly noon.

ELPIDI: *(Leans toward* RAISA*)* So there's Pushkin in this Turkish bath...

RAISA: *(Laughing like a horse)* I know what's coming. I know what's coming.

ELPIDI: So, there he is in this Turkish Bath....

ARISTARKH: Friends, comrades, let us say that we are sending Podsekalnikov to a better world, one from which no one returns.

WAITER: Is he going abroad?

ARISTARKH: Don't interrupt, please!

VOICE: Quiet! Quiet!

(Silence)

ELPIDI: So Pushkin takes off his underpants...

*(*RAISA *laughs like a horse.)*

VOICE: Quiet! Quiet!

RAISA: I can just see it!

ARISTARKH: Our dear Podsekalnikov— Yours is a beautiful and glorious decision. An example that others will one day follow!

RAISA: And the women who were working in the baths??

ARISTARKH: Because of you the Motherland will tremble, the gates of the Kremlin itself will fall off their hinges and the government as one body will come out to see what has happened and seeing what has happened it will hold out its hand to the merchant, and the merchant will hold out his hand to the worker, and the worker will hold out his hand to the factory worker and the factory worker will hold out his hand to the peasant and the peasant will hold out his hand to the landowner and the landowner will hold out his hand to...well you get the idea.

ELPIDI: So he says something that rhymes with....
(*Blows a raspberry*)

ARISTARKH: Glory belongs to you, Podsekalnikov.
To Podsekalnikov!

ALL: To Podsekalnikov!

ARISTARKH: To Podsekalnikov!

ALL: To Podsekalnikov!

ARISTARKH: To Podsekalnikov!

ALL: To Podsekalnikov!

SEMYON: To Podsekalnikov!

VOICES: Sh-sh. Sh-sh

ALEXANDER: Please, I ask for quiet! Quiet, please!
(*Silence*) Semyon, have you anything you wish to say?

SEMYON: Yes I do. What's the time?

MARGARITA: Don't think—drink!

ARISTARKH: (*Laughs, then sobs*) Look at me! When my
own mother died, not one tear. But now...but now...

PUGACHEV: I long for the day to see my government
hold out its hand to me.

RAISA: I long for the day to see my government hold its
hand around its throat.

SEMYON: What's the time? What's the time?

MARGARITA: Don't think—drink.

VIKTOR: I agree with most of what you said, Aristarkh
Dominikovich, but I would have said it differently. For
me, I would like to be in a fur coat, on the steppes, in a
wide sleigh, with church bells of Easter morning service
in the distance. On the back of my head is a gray beaver
cap, to the left and right of me are gypsies, on my lap is
my favorite dog. I would like the strings of my guitar to
break and to see the coachman sob into his homespun
mittens, I want to toss my cap away and fall into a

snowdrift and pray and curse and use bad language and then repent and then down a shot of ice cold vodka and whistle and give out a loud shout for the whole of the universe to hear and then I want to fly. To fly through Mother Russia with the earth spinning like a top under the runners of the sleigh, so that the horses spread themselves over the fields like they were birds! Faster horses, faster! Oh what magnificent horses they are. And my soul is tearing at me from the inside, in that distinctive Russian literary way; Faster! Faster? Where are we racing, Mother Russia! Where are we going? Faster! Oh where are we headed?!!!!

(EGOR *enters*)

EGOR: To prison, if you keep that up.

VIKTOR: Why to prison?

EGOR: Because you'd be breaking the speed limit.

VIKTOR: But it was just a metaphor.

EGOR: Then take my advice and keep your metaphors under the speed limit. ...So what about the shooting gallery? Is it going to be open or not?

ALEXANDER: We were just waiting for you, Egor. We started to think that you weren't coming.

MARGARITA: Put a smile on your lips, Egor.

EGOR: I never drink.

ALEXANDER: Never?

EGOR: I'm afraid I'd like it.

ALEXANDER: Why be afraid of that?

EGOR: What if I liked it and then all of a sudden the great communist revolution swept the world. Under the great communist revolutionary government there won't be any wine, so then what would I do?

MARGARITA: Just one tiny glass, for us ladies.

EGOR: That's another thing there won't be when the great revolution comes—there won't be any ladies.

PUGACHEV: That's ridiculous, a man can't live with a woman.

EGOR: There won't be any men either.

VIKTOR: No men? But what's left?

EGOR: Masses, masses and more masses. Enormous masses of masses.

ALEXANDER: Then, why don't you drink for the masses?

EGOR: Well, if it's for the masses, I can't exactly refuse. Can I? *(He takes a glass)* Tell me, writer, what do you write about?

VIKTOR: Everything.

EGOR: Everything, is it? Well Tolstoy wrote about everything and who reads him anymore. I'm a mailman and I want to read about mailmen, understand?

VIKTOR: I once wrote about an ironworks.

EGOR: Well then let the ironworkers read it. Mailmen aren't the slightest bit interested in iron workers. Let me say it again: I am a mailman and I want to read about mailmen, understand? So what do you think about that?

SEMYON: Egor, what do you think about life after death? A simple yes or no will suffice.

EGOR: I don't know about now, but after the great revolution there won't be any. I can promise you that.

MARGARITA: What are you standing up for, Semyon? Sit. Sit down and relax.

RAISA: *(At the table)* Oleg says: "Raisa, I can't get your stomach out of my head."

CLEOPATRA: Egor Timofeevich, you haven't seen much of life, have you? And by life I mean fine underwear, delicious furniture, furs, make-up.

MARGARITA: Don't eat, Semyon—drink.

ARISTARKH: Egor—just answer me one question: Who will make this great revolution you keep talking about?

EGOR: The same as who made our great revolution.

ARISTARKH: And who was that?

EGOR: Me. I mean, we.

ARISTARKH: I don't mean specifically, I mean in general. Here, I can show you what I'm getting at by way of an allegory.

EGOR: Please do.

ARISTARKH: The allegory of the beastly behavior of domestic animals.

EVERYONE: Quiet! Quiet!

MARGARITA: Don't listen, Semyon, drink.

ARISTARKH: There is a hen and she is tenderhearted. Under her were placed some duck eggs. And for many years she sat on them. For many years she warmed them with her body until they finally hatched. The ducks hatched from the eggs and triumphantly crawled out from under her, then they grabbed her by her neck and dragged her to the river. "What are you doing. I am your mother" cried the hen. "I'm the one who sat on you. What are you doing?" "Swim!" roared the ducks. Understand the allegory?

VOICES: Not really. I don't think so.

ARISTARKH: Well, who, in your opinion, is this hen? It is our great Liberal Cause. And who, in your opinion, are these eggs? These eggs are the proletariat. And for many years the Liberal Cause sat on the proletariat. She sat and sat until finally they hatched. Proletarians hatched from the eggs, grabbed the Liberal Cause and dragged it to the river. "We are your Mama", said the liberals, "We sat on you. What are you doing?" "Swim" roared the ducks. "I can't swim." "Then fly" "But a hen is not a bird", said the liberals. "Well, then sit!" And so the ducks sat the Liberal Cause down and gave it a little jacket which didn't allow any movement for the wings. And now its been almost five years that my brother-in-law has been sitting wearing a little white jacket with no room for his wings. Do you understand the allegory?

EGOR: What's to understand? Your brother-in-law embezzled money.

ARISTARKH: Of course, but that's not the point. What I am asking is, why did we sit on those eggs? Had we known then what we know now, we would have taken those eggs and.... What would you have done, Comrade Podsekalnikov?

SEMYON: Made eggnog.

ARISTARKH: You're a genius, Podsekalnikov. Truer words were never spoken.

CLEOPATRA: Is something troubling you, Semyon?

SEMYON: Well, now that you ask, I am sort of wondering whether there is life after death.

ALEXANDER: That's a question for the priest. He's the specialist on questions like that.

ELPIDI: How would you like me to respond: according to scripture or conscience?

SEMYON: What's the difference?

ELPIDI: Co-los-sal. I could also respond according to science as well. If you wish.

SEMYON: I just want the true answer, Father.

ELPIDI: According to religion—yes. According to science—no. According to conscience—could be.

SEMYON: Could be???

PUGACHEV: What are you asking him for? In about thirty minutes you'll find out for yourself.

SEMYON: In about what?? It's eleven thirty?! Why didn't somebody tell me?

MARGARITA: Don't think. Semyon, drink.

SEMYON: How could it be eleven thirty?!! It was just....
At my funeral. I want all of you to sing. Sing you
bastards! Sing your hearts out!!! Sure. I'll suffer for
you. I'll suffer for everybody! Because I'll be through
suffering for me... Listen to me. All of you. You want to
know when life begins? It begins, comrades...it began...
thirty minutes before death.... Keep listening to me...
I'm a dying man. And you want to know whose to
blame? They are. Whoever they are, they're the ones
to blame. Go up to any one of them and ask them:
"What have you done for Podsekalnikov?" And they
won't know what to say, because they aren't even
aware that within this Soviet Republic there exists a
Podsekalnikov! But there is a Podsekalnikov, comrades.
And I am him! And though they may not know that
yet, they soon will. If not in life, then I shall be known
in death! I will die, and when I am buried, then I shall
begin to speak. I will talk openly and boldly in the
name of everything and everyone. I will tell them that
I am dying for...for...that I am dying for...that I...God
damn it! How can I tell them what I'm dying for when
I haven't even read my suicide note?

ARISTARKH: That is easily fixed, Semyonovich. Bring in
an armchair and a table, Margarita.

MARGARITA: Waiter, a table.

(Table and an armchair brought in.)

ARISTARKH: Go ahead and read it, Podsekalnikov.

SEMYON: This is it?

ARISTARKH: Yes.

SEMYON: *(Reads)* "Why I do not have the strength to
live." I've been looking forward to reading this.

ARISTARKH: Sit and enjoy, Podsekalnikov. And,
remember, they are your words, now go ahead and
copy them.

SEMYON: *(Copying)* "Why I do not have the strength to live. People and members of the party, look history in the eye." Huh. Very nice. Very nice.

PUGACHEV: Friends, do you know what I think is the most beautiful thing in the world?

ALEXANDER: What?

PUGACHEV: Beauty. Beauty is so beautiful.

ALEXANDER: You're going to throw up, aren't you?

PUGACHEV: Me? I give it all to beauty.

SEMYON: *(Reads)* "Because we have all been touched by the purifying whirlwind of the revolution...." Exclamation mark. New paragraph. *(Copies)*

CLEOPATRA: I'm so bored with this gray life. If we weren't already in Moscow I'd say, let's go there.

SEMYON: *(Reads)* "Never forget that the Liberal Cause is the salt of our nation and, (God forbid) if it were ever extinguished, we wouldn't have any salt to season our lives." What do you know. *(Copies)* "Never forget...

VIKTOR: Aristarkh Dominikovich, the worm, which I spoke about, it is already here.

ARISTARKH: What?

VIKTOR: I told you yesterday about Fedia Pitnum—the go-getter? It looks like the worm, I'm afraid it's got him.

ARISTARKH: What is this worm you keep talking about? You're very gloomy, do you know that?

RAISA: I understand you've recently been abroad?

VIKTOR: Yes, I toured the workers' districts in France.

RAISA: Tell me, are large or small breasts fashionable this season in Paris?

VIKTOR: Either. Though large are more out, and small are more in.

CLEOPATRA: Paris, that civilized city: where what one is born with, one doesn't have to live with.

SEMYON: "Give all liberals their freedom to speak."

PUGACHEV: Give me a room with a bathtub.

SEMYON: Exclamation mark. "And that, comrades, is what I am dying for." Signature.

(PUGACHEV *begins to cry.*)

ALEXANDER: What's wrong? Why are you crying?

PUGACHEV: I'm homesick for my...for my native country.

ARISTARKH: For your native country? What country is that?

PUGACHEV: Russia!

SEMYON: My dear comrades—do you know what I can do?

VOICE: What's that?

SEMYON: No? Don't you know what I can do? Don't you? I can do whatever I want to do, comrades. Me. I don't have to be afraid of anyone ever again. Ever again. Because what can anyone do to me, I'm going to die anyway? I'm going to die anyway. See what I mean? Whatever I want to do, I can do. Anything I want, I can do. I'm afraid of nothing: Before I was afraid of everything, now—nothing! If I want to go to a meeting—any meeting, comrades and give the speaker—any speaker, comrades—the finger, I can. See, I can do everything. I'm afraid of no one. Here in the Soviet Union there are one hundred and forty million people and everybody is afraid of somebody, except me. I'm afraid of no one. No one. I'm going to die anyway! Comrades hold me down or I'm going to start dancing! Today I rule all the people. I am a dictator. I am a tzar! I can do everything! Whatever I want— I can do. Me, comrades.... So what should I do? How should I flex my muscles, comrades? What can I do, not for myself, but for the whole of humanity? I know what. I got it. I got it. Comrades I will call the Kremlin! I'll call direct to the Kremlin! The Kremlin—that pulsing red heart of the Soviet Union! Me—I will call...and I'll talk to someone...to someone...and I will curse him real good!! What do you say about that?! *(Goes to the telephone booth)*

ARISTARKH: For God's sake, Podsekalnikov!

CLEOPATRA: Don't do it, Semyon!

ELPIDI: What do you want to do that for?!

MARGARITA: Help!

SEMYON: Sh-sh! *(Takes off the receiver)* Silence! Two Colossuses are about to speak. Give me the Kremlin! Don't be afraid, don't be afraid, get it for me. Hello? Kremlin? Podsekalnikov here. Pod-se-kal-ni-kov. An individual. I said, an individual. An in-di-vid-u-al. *(Spells)* I-N-D-I-V-I-D-U-A-L. I want to talk to somebody. I don't care who, anybody; no—give me the most important person there. There's no *one* most important person??? Well, then you just tell them all that I have read Marx and I don't like Marx! Don't interrupt, I'm not finished yet. And you just tell them...that they can all just go to.... Hello? Hello? I don't believe it. *(Dumbfounded, drops the receiver)*

ARISTARKH: What happened?

SEMYON: They hung up.

VIKTOR: They did?

SEMYON: They hung up. They're afraid. They are afraid of me! Do you understand what this means?! The Kremlin is afraid of me. Of what I represent, comrades. God, it scares you just to think about it. Of me. Ever since I was a little boy, I've wanted to be a genius, but my parents were against it. Up to now what have I been? I've been a statistic. Oh life, how you've made fun of me! Oh life, for all those years you've been insulting me! But at last, my hour has come. Oh life now I demand satisfaction!

(Clock strikes twelve. Silence)

SEMYON: Maybe it's fast.

(Pause. Everyone but SEMYON sits.)

ARISTARKH: Let's all sit quietly for a moment.

SEMYON: Well, then farewell, comrades. *(Starts to leave, returns, takes a bottle and hides it in his pocket.)* For courage. *(Starts to go)*

(WAITER enters.)

WAITER: Come back and see us again, Semyon.

SEMYON: No, now you come to me. *(Leaves)*

(Curtain)

END OF ACT THREE

ACT FOUR

(A room in SEMYON's *apartment)*

*(*SERAFIMA *beats eggnog in a glass.)*

SERAFIMA: *(Sings)* The tempest storms
The rain falls loud
As lightning lights the, sky!
The thunder roars
The tempest storms
Where we young men do lie.

MASHA: *(From the next room)* The thunder roars
The tempest storms
Where we young men do lie.

SERAFIMA: *(Sings)* But do not weep...

MASHA: Mama! Mama!

SERAFIMA: What is it?

*(*MASHA *enters with a kerosene lamp. In the glass lamp is a curling iron.)*

MASHA: What do you think Semyon would like better: curls or waves?

SERAFIMA: With him, who can guess, Masha?

MASHA: So what do I do?

SERAFIMA: Curl the front and wave the back, that way you can't lose. *(Sings)*
But do not weep...

MASHA: He'll be back any minute, Mama—hurry!

SERAFIMA: Hurry? How much faster can I work?
I've already beaten up a glass's worth.

MASHA: He sure is crazy about his egg nog.

SERAFIMA: He's deserved it today. *(Sings)*
But do not weep
For we but sleep...

MASHA: Do you think he'll get the job, Mama?

SERAFIMA: Why wouldn't he get the job?

MASHA: If he doesn't get the job, I think that'll be it,
Mama.

SERAFIMA: What's hard to understand is why there
aren't enough jobs for everyone! All you have to do
is look around Russia and you can see that it needs
all the help it can get.

MASHA: So then why isn't everyone working?

SERAFIMA: I think it's because of the system.

MASHA: The system? What system is that?

SERAFIMA: The system where if everybody had a job,
then those people whose job it is to give other people
jobs would themselves be out of a job. And if that were
to happen then almost everybody would be out of
work, because the most popular job today is the job
of giving other people jobs.

MASHA: Oh, that system... We are soon going to be
happy again, aren't we, Mama?

SERAFIMA: We are soon going to be happy again. *(Sings)*
My voice will sound
As I fire each round
Give me my Glory and Death.

MASHA: *(Sings)* My voice will sound
As I fire each round
Give me my Glory and Death.

BOTH: *(Sing)* Give me my Glory and Death.

MASHA: What's this letter doing here?

SERAFIMA: Must be an old one, throw it out.

MASHA: No, it's sealed. And it's addressed to you.

SERAFIMA: To me? Who would be writing me? Read it, Masha.

MASHA: *(Reads)* "Dear mother-in-law, by the time you read this letter, I won't be alive anymore. Break this news to Masha gently."

SERAFIMA: Oh God!

MASHA: Wait! *(Reads)* "My coat and cigarette case I leave to my brother in Yeletz. Semyon." I don't believe it. How could he?!!! Oh God oh God! *(She falls onto the bed and sobs.)*

SERAFIMA: Masha! Masha! Don't cry. Please, don't cry! You mustn't cry!

(ARISTARKH, ELPIDI, MARGARITA, ALEXANDER, and SEAMSTRESS enter.)

ELPIDI: Weep, weep; widow Podsekalnikov. Embrace your children and cry out "Where is your Daddy? Your Daddy is gone. There is no Daddy and no more shall there be."

ALEXANDER: There never was.

ELPIDI: What?

ALEXANDER: There never was a Daddy.

ELPIDI: Why?

ALEXANDER: Because there weren't any children.

ELPIDI: Oh. Weep, weep, widow Podsekalnikov for the children that might have been!

ARISTARKH: Father, let me handle this widow. Podsekalnikov, sometimes out of sadness comes no sadness; sometimes out of sorrow there comes no sorrow; your husband is now lifeless but, I say, let him

live in the hearts of all Russian liberals! His body is now
cold but let him begin to warm our lives! Feel better?

SEAMSTRESS: Allow me to suggest a felt hat, widow
Podsekalnikov. Without losing its basic appeal of being
quite tasteful, felt has become over the last few years
rather fashionable. And fashion and taste are the two
elements one ought to consider when dressing for a
funeral. Of course, if you prefer straw, I can't stop you.
(Hands her a felt hat)

MASHA: I don't need anything! Leave me alone!
Why did he do it?!

MARGARITA: Masha, is this any way to behave?!
Don't you care about how you look? You want to
look like a rag at the funeral?

SERAFIMA: The funeral? But we don't have the money
to bury him.

ARISTARKH: Leave all that to us. Funeral costs,
mourning clothes, caskets—these little burdens
we Liberals have learned to bear with a smile.

SEAMSTRESS: Shall we begin the fitting, widow
Podsekalnikov?

MASHA: I can't...leave me alone! How will I go on
living?!! *(Puts on the hat)*

ARISTARKH: You shall live as your husband died—
as a human being who is alone, totally, completely,
desperately, alone, living and then dying for what
you believe.

SEAMSTRESS: The front's forty one.

ARISTARKH: And in your aloneness as he was in his,
you will find comfort, and strength.

SEAMSTRESS: The back's ninety four.

ARISTARKH: For it takes strength to walk, as he did,
down the bumpy road that is our Liberal Cause.
And that is where he lies today.

SERAFIMA: He's lying in the middle of the road?

ARISTARKH: In the middle of the road of history.

SERAFIMA: Is that in Moscow?

ARISTARKH: And he shall remain there as an awesome reminder for those who follow.

SEAMSTRESS: How about a little shirring?

ARISTARKH: And as future generations march along this road, they shall trip and stumble over the body of your husband and they will stop and ask....

SEAMSTRESS: Would you mind raising your arm?

ARISTARKH: "Whose body is this that we tripped over?" And we shall reply—

SEAMSTRESS: Crimped or flared?

ARISTARKH: "This is Podsekalnikov. He dared to ask the great question!"

MASHA: Is it possible to have it both crimped and flared?

ARISTARKH: Honor and glory to the husband of the widow Podsekalnikov. Honor and glory to the wife of our much lamented deceased.

SERAFIMA: Where did you say he was?

ARISTARKH: I don't know. You'd better ask the police. We'll leave you now, widow Podsekalnikov, but we will be back. You shall not be deserted in this, your time of need. Look at me. Not a tear when my own Mother died, but now...but now... *(Sobs)*

(Kisses her on the cheek. They start to leave. ALEXANDER *goes to kiss her.)*

ALEXANDER: Not the cheek, Masha...but your eyes that tear... *(Kisses her eyes)* ...and your lips that tremble... *(Kisses her lips)*

MARGARITA: Alexander!

(They leave.)

SERAFIMA: They sure are nice people. And, at times like these; it's nice to know that there still are nice people in the world.

MASHA: I'd rather know that Semyon was still in this world.

SERAFIMA: It's hard to believe, isn't it? He's gone! Our beloved is gone!! What time is your fitting?

MASHA: Today at three. At her shop. Here's the address on the card.

SERAFIMA: Dressmaking atelier, Madam Sophie. Sounds expensive.

MASHA: You can tell she's not cheap by the way she acts.

SERAFIMA: Shouldn't you take off your hat, Masha? You don't want to wear it out.

MASHA: Let it wear out! Why should I care?! Why should I care about anything anymore?! Why should I care if I live or die. We're cursed Mama! That's what we are! This morning I had Semyon, just this morning, but then I didn't have a hat. Now I have a hat, but no Semyon.... I'm beginning to think there's no such thing as total happiness.

(Knock at the door)

SERAFIMA: Who's there?

MASHA: Mama! Oh God!

(Two suspicious-looking men carry in the lifeless body of SEMYON.*)*

SERAFIMA: Holy saints! Here, put him down, over here! Over here!

MASHA: Semyon, what have you done?! Semyon!!

FIRST MAN: It not so much what he's done, I think, as what he's not doing.

SECOND MAN: It happened like that.

SERAFIMA: You saw it?

SECOND MAN: Didn't miss a thing.

FIRST MAN: At first we don't really notice him, but then he says: "Take me to this address." Then he goes behind a tree, and he stands there for a while, and then, bang, and he's down. We run to him, but we're too late. There he is on the ground, without a peep coming out of him.

SECOND MAN: I think he'd reached his limit.

(MASHA *is sobbing.*)

(*They leave.*)

MASHA: If only we hadn't let you out of our sight— then you wouldn't be dead!

SEMYON: Dead? Who's dead? I'm dead? Hold me!

BOTH WOMEN: Help!

SEMYON: Hold me! Hold me! I'm flying! I'm flying! Hosanna! Hosanna!

MASHA: Semyon! Semyon!

SERAFIMA: Semyon!

SEMYON: I hear my name. Who's there? Who calls Semyon?

MASHA: It's me.

SEMYON: It's you?

MASHA: It's me, Masha.

SEMYON: Masha? Which Masha?

MASHA: Which Masha? How many Mashas do you know? Look, Semyon, you've escaped. God is with you.

SEMYON: God is with me? Oh, I apologize. I did not recognize you. Allow me to introduce myself, I am the soul of Podsekalnikov.

MASHA: He's lost his mind, Mama.

SERAFIMA: Semyon, where have you been? What have you been doing?

SEMYON: I come from a city called Moscow, Father, and there I have spent my days doing good works, lots and lots of good works.

MASHA: Semyon!

SEMYON: Not to brag, Father, but I do think I have all the makings of a good soul for the Heavenly City of God. I'm great at taking orders and I'll never question anything you say. I've spent my life taking orders and never questioning what anyone said. And that's not all, I can dance, I can sing: *(Sings)* "Glory Be to God in Heaven and on Earth!"

SERAFIMA: Come to your senses!

SEMYON: And if there's a piano around I could learn to play the tuba, Father.

SERAFIMA: I am not a Father, I am a mother-in-law, Semyon!

SEMYON: A what?

SERAFIMA: A mother-in-law! A mother-in-law! Your mother-in-law!

SEMYON: My mother-in-law? Really? Well, what do you know? When did you croak?

MASHA: He's delirious. He must have wounded himself.... *(Bends over him)* Semyon, my pigeon, you are wounded!

SERAFIMA: What is it?

MASHA: Smell him.

SERAFIMA: Wonderful! He's so high no wonder he thinks he's in Heaven. We should have guessed.

SEMYON: Do you happen to know where one applies to be considered for the heavenly hosts?

MASHA: Sober him up!

SERAFIMA: Get the pitcher and pour it over his head. Keep pouring! More. Let him think his sins are being washed away!

SEMYON: Ahhhhh!! Where am I...? Is this the world of the flesh or of the spirit?

SERAFIMA: The flesh, the flesh.

MASHA: What the hell were you doing, leaving a note that you were going to shoot yourself and then going out and getting pickled?! You bastard! You almost gave me a stroke! Here I am weeping my eyes out, sobbing uncontrollably.... Ask her, ask her, wasn't I sobbing uncontrollably? Me, what with my anemia!

SEMYON: Wait!

MASHA: No, you wait! Here I am weeping my eyes out, sobbing uncontrollably, in spite of my anemia, acting my role of the grieving widow, and you're not even dead, just drunk! What are you trying to do, kill me?! Is that what you'd like?! Well, answer me! I'm asking you a question, so answer me!!!!

SEMYON: Wait! What time is it?

MASHA: It's two o'clock.

SEMYON: Two o'clock! How could it be two?! I was supposed to do it at twelve, at twelve, Masha! What time did I come home?

MASHA: You mean what time were you dragged home.

SEMYON: I was dragged? Who dragged me?

SERAFIMA: Two strange men.

SEMYON: Two men?... That's right, I was sitting with two men on a curb, we were drinking together from the bottle....

MASHA: So now you drink right from the bottle! How disgusting!

SEMYON: Has anyone else come by?

SERAFIMA: Some very well-dressed people were here.

SEMYON: And what did they want?

SERAFIMA: They came to offer their sympathies.

MASHA: They said they'd pay for everything, because my husband died a hero.

SERAFIMA: How embarrassing! What will they think?!

MASHA: One thing's for sure, they'll demand that we pay back every penny they've spent.

SERAFIMA: At this very moment, your mourning dress is probably being worked on. And that seamstress, Madam Sophie, I'm sure she doesn't come cheap.

MASHA: Maybe they haven't started yet. We better go and see. Let's go, Mama.

SEMYON: Wait. There's a chance I still might shoot myself.

MASHA: Right. Let's go, Mama.

SEMYON: I will shoot myself. You'll see. I'll do it! I'll do it!

SERAFIMA: Shoot yourself? You? You couldn't even be hit by a truck.

(They leave.)

SEMYON: They don't believe me. They don't believe me. Even Masha, my own wife, doesn't believe me. Alright, I'll show them and won't they be sorry. Won't everybody be sorry. Where is it? Here. *(Takes out the revolver)* Just got to do it once, without thinking, directly into the heart and then—immediate death. *(Places revolver to his chest)* On the other hand, maybe the mouth would be better. Be quicker in the mouth. *(Puts revolver into his mouth and then removes it)* I'll count to three. *(Puts it into the mouth again)* Ua...tua... *(Removes it)* Maybe I should count to a thousand. *(Puts it into his*

mouth) Ua...tua...ee...fou...fi...si...se...eigh... *(Takes it out)*
If I'm going to count, it'd make more sense to shoot
myself in the chest. *(Puts revolver to his chest)* One, two,
three, four, five, six, seven, eight, nine...only a coward
would count to a thousand...look, just do it once...
without thinking...directly into the heart and....
I'll count to a hundred. One hundred and that's it.
No more... No! Fifteen, that's quicker. Right, so it's
fifteen... *(Revolver to his chest)* One, two, three, four, five,
six, seven, eight, nine, ten...eleven...twelve...thirteen...
fourteen...what am I wasting all this time counting for?
What is there—some kind of rule that says you have to
count? I'll do it in the mouth then, if I'm not counting....
(Puts it in the month, takes it out) Where will the bullet
go? Right here. Into the head. I sort of feel sorry for the
head. After all my face is on this head. So it's the heart,
and that's final. But first I have to find out where it is.
Where it beats is where it is. That's where I'll aim.
There. There's where it's beating. And here. It's beating
here, too. And here, too. What a big heart I've got.
No matter where I touch—it's beating. And how it's
beating. It feels like it's about to burst. It's going to
burst any second! It can't do that—if I die from a heart
attack I won't have time to shoot myself! I can't die yet!
I have to live! Live, live, live! So I can shoot myself!
I'm not going to make it. I'll suffocate. I've got a minute,
maybe a minute left. So shoot—shoot anywhere, just
shoot!! *(Revolver drops out of his hand)* Too late, I'm
dying...who's there??!!!

(A BOY *with a number of wreaths enters. They are wrapped
in paper.)*

BOY: Does the deceased live here?

SEMYON: Who?

BOY: The deceased, does he live here?

SEMYON: Who are you? What do you want?

BOY: I'm from the World Beyond.

SEMYON: What do you mean you're from the World Beyond?

BOY: The World Beyond Funeral Home. I'm supposed to deliver these. *(Sets up the wreaths)*

SEMYON: Who sent them?

(BOY removes the wrappers, SEMYON reads the inscriptions.)

SEMYON: "Sleep peacefully, Semyon Podsekalnikov. You are a hero...", "Respectful admirers of your death.", "To an unforgettable son-in-law—your mother-in-law."

BOY: Are the wreaths for you?

SEMYON: Yes, for me...I mean, for us, yes.

BOY: Sign here. *(Hands him a book)* No, right here.

SEMYON: *(Reads)* Six funeral wreaths. *(Signs)*

BOY: Good-bye. *(Leaves)*

SEMYON: *(Goes up to the wreaths, straightens a ribbon, reads)* "Don't say he's dead, because he lives— Your Raisa." Oh my God, she knows! That bitch, how did she guess? Where's the revolver? Hurry! *(Raises the revolver)* So he lives, does he? Well, take a look at how he lives. Here look. *(Places the revolver to his temple)* Sleep peacefully, Semyon Podsekalnikov, you are a hero. You are a hero. You are a hero, Podsekalnikov, so sleep... *(Drops his arm)* So I'm a hero who can't sleep. And why can't I sleep? Because I'm too tired. I'm very, very tired. Maybe if I rested for a bit. Maybe if I sit and relax and read the paper for a while... Renew my strength... Yes, yes. *(Sits down, takes a paper, reads)* Foreign affairs. Foreign affairs... how trivial they are when compared to the affairs of one man. *(Turns a page, reads)* "At the corner of Semyonovsky and Barabanny Streets an unidentified man was crushed to death by a falling brick." God, how lucky can you get. He just walks along, not a thought in his head and then like that

it happens. Whereas I think and think and think and
it doesn't happen. Maybe that's the problem—I'm
thinking too much. That's it! That's why! Of course!
I just have to get a hold of myself and think about
something else, get into the mood of what I'm thinking
about and then—it's over. I just have to think about
something wonderful and beautiful, something striking
and here I am walking along, my mind in the clouds,
maybe I'm singing something. Yes, I'm singing:
Kiss me, Mama,
Your kisses are true.
Kiss me Papa,
Your kisses are glue.
Kiss me Sister
Your kisses are new.
So when I get older
I'll know what to do.
(Brings his outstretched arm with the revolver to his temple)
Kiss me Mama,
Your kisses are...
(Stops his hand)
Your kisses are.... I can't....
Your kisses are.... I...
So when I get older
I'll...I'll... I can't! Damn it! I can't!!!!

VOICES: Careful! Careful! Watch the door! Watch it!
Turn it around! Turn it around.

(MEN enter carrying in a coffin.)

MAN: Towards you! Towards you, just a little!
Don't push! There. Set it on the table.

(They place the coffin on the table.)

MAN: There. It's delivered.

SEMYON: Thank you. Thank you very much.

MAN: He's here?

SEMYON: Who's here?

MAN: Podsekalnikov. The deceased.

SEMYON: Oh him. Yes, he's around somewhere.

MAN: Where?

SEMYON: Where? Oh, you know, around. I mean, he's not here yet, but we expect him any minute now.

MAN: Was it a difficult death?

SEMYON: That, I think, would be an understatement.

MAN: Our sympathies. Goodbye.

(They leave.)

(For a few moments, SEMYON remains completely still. He goes toward the coffin, walks around, peeks inside, straightens the pillow and places the wreathes around the coffin. Then he pulls out the revolver and places the muzzle to his temple. Drops his arm. Approaches the mirror, covers it with black cloth. Again places the muzzle to his temple, closes his eyes. Listens. Opens his eyes; goes to the clock, climbs on a chair, stops the pendulum. Again places the muzzle to his temple. Pause)

SEMYON: Why haven't the scientists figured out a way for a man to shoot himself without feeling anything? What about chloroform? For example, to take but one example, I think it's at least worth looking into. And they say they work for the good the humanity. Well, I'm human, what about my good?! They call themselves healers of the sick, givers of life. So give me the strength so I can kill myself!!!!

(MASHA and SERAFIMA run in.)

MASHA: They're coming!

SEMYON: Who's coming?

MASHA: Everybody's coming!

(They run out of the room.)

(SEMYON rushes around the room. Noise of a crowd outside)

SEMYON: Oh God! Oh God!

(*Noise gets louder*)

SEMYON: Oh God! (*Jumps on the table*) Oh God!
(*Jumps into the coffin*)

(*Noise nearer*)

SEMYON: I'll wait in here, until everybody leaves,
and then...then I'll do it. (*Stretches out in the coffin.*)

(ARISTARKH, PUGACHEV, ALEXANDER, MARGARITA,
RAISA, ELPIDI, EGOR *enter. Everyone in mourning, many
hold flowers.* MASHA *and* SERAFIMA—*with their backs to
the audience—are terrified and try to hold back the crowd.*)

MASHA: Put yourself in his place. People don't want
to die. Who wants to die? And who can be blamed for
that?

ARISTARKH: We know who's to be blamed! And thanks
to your late husband we'll name names!

SERAFIMA: You don't understand, he's not....

MASHA: Look, what about me? You don't think I knew,
do you? Because I didn't. I swear I didn't. He'll tell you
himself. He will. Semyon! Sem... (*Sees* SEMYON)
Ahhhhh!!!!!

ARISTARKH: Quick, Egor, a chair!

SERAFIMA: What's wrong? What's wrong?

MASHA: It's him!

SERAFIMA: It's who?

MASHA: It's...

SERAFIMA: Ahhhhh!!!! (*Sees* SEMYON)

ARISTARKH: Quick, Egor, another chair!

(EGOR *brings chairs.*)

MARGARITA: He looks almost alive.

ELPIDI: Though the nose is a bit bigger.

MASHA: Let me up. Let me up. He's not dead,
he's drunk. He'll sleep it off and then get up!

EGOR: He won't get up.

MASHA: He will get up! He's alive! I know he's alive!

RAISA: Listen how she screams.

MARGARITA: She's out of her mind.

ARISTARKH: Take her to the next room, Egor.

MASHA: Semyon! Semyon!

SERAFIMA: Wake up, Semyon, wake up!

RAISA: The old woman's gone too.

ARISTARKH: Take them both into the next room, Egor.

MASHA: He's alive! He's alive!

(EGOR *takes them both off.*)

RAISA: How she carries on.

MARGARITA: Just listen to her.

MASHA'S VOICE: He's alive! He's alive!

RAISA: Poor thing.

MARGARITA: She's taking it hard.

RAISA: Quite a scene. Maybe we should go and watch.

MARGARITA: You mean—help.

RAISA: Of course. Help. Maybe we should go and help.

MARGARITA: What are friends for?

(*They hurry out.*)

ALEXANDER: Pardon my indiscretion, comrades,
but when do you intend to settle our business?

PUGACHEV: What business is that?

ALEXANDER: I've handed over the body, now you hand
over the money.

ARISTARKH: Don't you believe in anything but money,
comrade Petrovich?

ALEXANDER: I believe what I can eat.

ARISTARKH: But ideas feed the mind, comrade; they feed up hope.

ALEXANDER: Better a few less ideas and a little more bread. Let's settle our business.

ARISTARKH: We'll settle when you've done everything you agreed to do.

ALEXANDER: What do you mean?

ARISTARKH: Have you made copies of the suicide note?

ALEXANDER: The typist is still working on it now.

ARISTARKH: Then start distributing them. The shot's been fired, now let the world hear it.

ELPIDI: Then you're hoping for great repercussions?

ARISTARKH: I am hoping, yes, though I am also a little bit afraid. Our deceased, unfortunately, was not a very remarkable man. Now if Gorky or a People's Commissar had shot himself, I'd feel a lot better.

SEMYON: *(In the coffin)* So would I.

VIKTOR: I disagree. For us, who the deceased was, is not what's important. It's not the meal that matters, but how you serve it up. I had a talk with Fedia Petunin yesterday. I told him about a certain Podsekalnikov. I made up everything. Petunin fell in love with him. So now that this Podsekalnikov is dead who's to know the difference. Who's to know the difference between fact and fiction? Whatever people believe, that's what truth is. So it's not the fact of a death that will ignite the people, it's what we make up about that death.

ARISTARKH: We must get the people whispering. That's the first step.

ELPIDI: We'll lay him out in the chapel and arrange a number of farewell services.

ARISTARKH: Good idea.

(Others return, holding up MASHA and SERAFIMA.)

ARISTARKH: I think we should begin, Father.

ELPIDI: Yes, let us begin.

MASHA: Let me go! Let me go!

ELPIDI: The Lord bless us and blessed be the Lord....

OTHERS: Amen.

MASHA: Don't you know what you're doing? He's alive!

ELPIDI: Grant us thy peace, O Lord...

MASHA: Stop this! Stop it!

SERAFIMA: Help!

ELPIDI: Lord have mercy upon us...

OTHERS: Lord have mercy upon us...

ELPIDI: And grant us Thy peace...

OTHERS: And grant us Thy peace. Amen.

(Deaf and dumb BOY *peeks through the door.)*

MARGARITA: You want to see him? Don't be shy, come in. Come in.

(He comes in and takes his place near the coffin.)

ELPIDI: Lord have mercy upon us...

MASHA: Police!

ELPIDI: ...and Grant the glory of everlasting peace to Thy servant, Semyon...

MASHA: Police!

ELPIDI: The window, close the window, quick!... Lord have mercy upon us and grant him eternal rest....

OTHERS: Lord, have mercy upon us.

ARISTARKH: Excuse me, Father. I know the Word of God is sacred, but considering the situation, I wonder if we couldn't hurry things up a bit.

ELPIDI: I see your point.... Lord have mercy upon us.

OTHERS: Lord have mercy upon us.

MASHA: He's alive!

SERAFIMA: Wake him up!

ELPIDI: And deliver us, O Lord, from suffering, hatred and want...

OTHERS: And want...

MASHA: Why doesn't he wake up? Mama, maybe he's really dead.

ELPIDI: And rest his soul with the saints...

OTHERS: And rest his soul...

MASHA: Ahhhhhhhh!!!

VOICES: She's fainted. Water! Water!

(Everyone rushes to MASHA. *Only the deaf and dumb* BOY *remains by the coffin. He kneels.* SEMYON *sits up and rubs his tearful eyes with a handkerchief. The* BOY *stands up, makes a sign of the cross, he throws back his head and sees* SEMYON. *The* BOY *cries out and falls flat on his back.)*

VOICES: What's happened? Another one!

ARISTARKH: Quick, carry him out. Carry him out!

(The men carry out the coffin.)

MASHA: He's dead. I know he's dead...

*(*BOY *runs to her, horrified, he gestures about what he has just seen. He takes out his handkerchief and brushes his eyes, just as* SEMYON *did.)*

MASHA: You feel sorry for him too? You're crying. I couldn't even begin to tell you how unhappy I am. *(She embraces the boy.)*

(Curtain)

END OF ACT FOUR

ACT FIVE

(A cemetery. Near piles of dirt is a freshly dug grave.)

CLEOPATRA: *(Running in, dragging OLEG behind her)*
Look here!

OLEG: Look where?

CLEOPATRA: Here!

OLEG: Where?

CLEOPATRA: Here! This is where they'll bury him.

OLEG: Bury who?

CLEOPATRA: Oleg, I have a confession to make....
I am a murderess! I am a murderess, Oleg! Oleg!
Hold me. I am afraid.

OLEG: Kapushka, what are you talking about?

CLEOPATRA: Oleg, you are different, you won't judge
me. Oleg, I killed him!

OLEG: Who?!

CLEOPATRA: Podsekalnikov! Oleg, he wanted my body;
he wanted—me—all of me, but I said—No!—and then
he killed himself over me.

OLEG: On top of you?

CLEOPATRA: Because of me! Oleg, I am a murderess!
I am afraid, Oleg. Take me to your place!

OLEG: I'd better take you home.

(She cries.)

(Two old women walk past the grave.)

FIRST: I'm such an old fool!

SECOND: Why is that?

FIRST: How could I have missed it? There's a new one just dug and I missed it.

SECOND: I saw it on my way to church this morning.

FIRST: Who's passed away?

SECOND: A man from the parish. Serafima's son-in-law, Podsekalnikov.

(CLEOPATRA *wails.*)

FIRST: I just don't understand how I could have missed it.

SECOND: They layed him out for two days in the chapel. I went to look at him with Pankratyevna.

FIRST: Pankratyevna? She saw him too? Am I the only one who missed it?

SECOND: How we cried! Both of us! (*She cries.*)

FIRST: Will somebody please tell me how I missed it?!!!

(*She cries. So all three women are crying.* ALEXANDER *and* ARISTARKH *run in.*)

ALEXANDER: It looks best from over here. Over here. Well, how do you like it?

ARISTARKH: Not a bad choice. (*Wipes his eyes*)

ALEXANDER: I chose it as if I were choosing my own.

(ALEXANDER *cries.* OLEG *looks at all five of them who are now crying.* VIKTOR *runs in.*)

VIKTOR: Have the invitations gone out?

ALEXANDER: They're out.

VIKTOR: We forgot someone.

ARISTARKH: Who's that?

VIKTOR: Fedia Pitunin. He should have been invited.

ARISTARKH: How could you forget him?

VIKTOR: I've had other things on my mind. And I haven't run into him for two days, if I had I would have remembered.

ARISTARKH: Well, it's not that important.

VIKTOR: No? So then what's important?

ARISTARKH: Getting the people to speak their minds!!!!

FIRST: How did he die?

SECOND: Did himself in.

FIRST: Oh, how horrible. How could I have missed it? Why did he do himself in? Do we know?

SECOND: It's certainly no secret.

FIRST: No?... Tell me... Really?... What a shame... How interesting... It always comes down to that.

(They leave.)

ARISTARKH: Did you hear that? The people have begun to whisper!!!!!

(They run out.)

CLEOPATRA: Oleg, you don't know what I've been through: my Mama was a gypsy. Her body drove men crazy. When I became fifteen, I was like Mama. Once I was in a cab, on my way to buy some slippers—and do you know what happened—the shoe clerk in the store couldn't control himself and bit my foot—I needed ten stitches! From that moment on I have hated men. Then it was a foreigner. Next, a communist. Then a pilot, I laughed in his face and he flew over the city and circled until he crashed. And now there is Podsekalnikov! Women threw themselves at him like moths before a flame. Raisa chewed up a glass because of him, but he only wanted me. Only me! But I said—No! No! Podsekalnikov, back! Back! Then suddenly—bang, and there was no more Podsekalnikov. Oleg, I hate my body, it frightens me. I don't want to be alone with it anymore. Take my body, Oleg, take it—get it away from me!

OLEG: Kapocha the thing is....

CLEOPATRA: Hold me, Oleg. I feel faint! I'm getting weak. It's more than I can take.... Tighter! Tighter!... Let me go! Let me go! Alright, I'll go.

OLEG: Go where?

CLEOPATRA: To your place.

OLEG: Kapochka, don't misunderstand me...but today is sort of...inconvenient for me. The thing is....

CLEOPATRA: I understand. Don't say another word. You have Raisa. You've made your choice; I won't beg, Oleg. But let me ask you just one thing: What do you have when you have Raisa? You have a stomach...just a stomach. But can a stomach laugh, Oleg? Can it sing, can it smile? No, Oleg, and even if hers could it'd be pretty disgusting. Think about that, Oleg. Think about whose Mama was a gypsy. Think about what I say. Let's go to your place so you can think about it.

OLEG: Kapochka, it's just that today is sort of inconvenient...

CLEOPATRA: I see. In that case, Oleg, I know what I must do. Farewell! *(Runs off)*

OLEG: Kapochka! Kapochka!

(Shakes his head and walks after her, doffs his hat as the funeral procession enters, and follows her off.)

ARISTARKH: Careful. Careful.

ALEXANDER: Don't push, please, don't push the widow.

EGOR: Pushy. Pushy.

FIRST: Young man, you are talking to a grandmother!

EGOR: You're Semyon's grandmother?

FIRST: Not his, but that doesn't mean I don't want to see.

EGOR: See whatever you can from there; just stay out of our way.

PUGACHEV: Lower the coffin!

VIKTOR: Who's making a speech in the name of the masses?

ARISTARKH: Egor. Go ahead, Egor.

EGOR: I'm scared to.

ARISTARKH: Scared about what? What's scary about a funeral oration?

EGOR: Words. Words are scary. They're like sparrows, once you let them go you can never get them back, and whatever you can't get back can be used against you.

ARISTARKH: But we agreed, Egor.

EGOR: So—I changed my mind. Anyway, I don't know how to begin.

VIKTOR: How about beginning with: "Something is rotten in the state of Denmark..."?

EGOR: Who said that?

VIKTOR: Shakespeare.

EGOR: Why didn't you say that before?! *(Runs to the mound of earth)* Comrades, please, let the orator speak!... Comrades, I have joyful news to share with you. Just a moment ago I received news from comrade Shakespeare that all is not well in the state of Denmark. This was, of course, to be expected. The rotten system of capitalism has once again revealed itself! Why are you tugging at me?

VIKTOR: Egor, talk about the deceased.

EGOR: I'm getting to him. And so, comrades, though all is not well in Denmark, and for that we may rejoice, we must not rejoice too much because one of us had died. On the other hand, though one of us has died we must not feel too sad today, because all is not well in the state of Denmark! Why are you tugging at me?!

(He is pulled off the mound)

VOICES: What's happening? What's going on?!

ALEXANDER: Dear friends, our comrade has taken ill! He can't go on, the wound is too fresh, the loss too great—he is choked with tears.

MASHA: Why am I still alive?! I want to die! I want to die!

MARGARITA: Later. Later. Sh-sh.

VIKTOR: Drink what you want,
Curse as you will,
He's paid the price,
He's picked up our bill.
His life was a great song,
Our's is a bad poem.

Once it was joyful
Yes, once it was grand,
To lie in the grass,
Or stick my toes in the sand.
But from this time forth,
Wherever my way shall wind,
I'll just be alone
Passing the time.
His life was a great song,
Ours is a bad poem.

Which path shall I follow,
What road do I take?
He never asked these questions,
He never was a fake.
He drank as he wanted
He cursed as he willed,
He paid his own price,
He picked up his own bill.

His life was a great song,
Ours is a bad poem.

RAISA: Very subtle.

EGOR: Now it's my turn. I want to read something.

ALEXANDER: Hold him down! Hold him down!

EGOR: Let go of me! *(Runs to the mound)* I'm going
to read a poem I wrote myself about death and the
masses. You, Masha, look at me. See my hand? When
I wave this hand you say: "who?" Do you understand?
Like this.

MASHA: *(Through tears)* Who?

EGOR: Not yet!.. You ready? Then I'll begin. Verses on
death and the masses. *(Moves his hand)*

MASHA: Who?

EGOR: That wasn't a wave, that was an itch!

CROWD: Sh-sh. Quiet!

EGOR: Had he but lived in this world
And worked in a State Institution
He would have been more equal than
The other equals... *(Waves his hand)*

MASHA: Who?

EGOR: Semyon Podsekalnikov!!! Very nice. *(Continues)*
Had he but lived in...

(CLEOPATRA runs in followed by OLEG.)

OLEG: Kapochka!

RAISA: Oleg!

OLEG: Raisa!

MASHA: Who?

CLEOPATRA: Don't try to stop me!

VOICES: Who's trying to stop her? Who is she? Must be
a relative.

CLEOPATRA: I'm not here to say farewell, but rather that I'm coming with you.

VOICE: I think she's crazy.

CLEOPATRA: You killed yourself over me, now I know what I have to do.

VOICES: I hope she means because of her.

MASHA: Excuse me, I think you've made a mistake, this is my husband.

CLEOPATRA: Wives are always the last to know. He wanted me. He wanted all of me! But I kept saying No!

RAISA: She's lying. I'm the one who said "no"!

CLEOPATRA: You? You don't even know the meaning of the word.

RAISA: He loved my stomach!

CLEOPATRA: He wanted my body!

ARISTARKH: Please, comrades, please! This little personal drama here, is but one example of the mistrust and animosity that has surrounded the Russian Liberal Cause...

VIKTOR: Shut up. The deceased played the tuba. He was an artist! He wanted....

CLEOPATRA: ...my body!!!!

PUGACHEV: Meat! Meat! Comrades, meat! I'm a butcher but you try to run my shop in times like these! I have no strength left. Everyone wants to see my books! Nobody trusts anyone anymore. That's why people are shooting themselves!

ARISTARKH: That's no reason to shoot yourself! I was his friend, and only those close to him can answer Why? Why he killed himself!

SERAFIMA: Because of liver sausage.

PUGACHEV: Because of liver sausage? Of course! Meat! Meat!

RAISA: Because of me!

CLEOPATRA: My body! My body!

ELPIDI: The church! The church!

PUGACHEV: Meat! Meat!

ARISTARKH: Comrades! Comrades!

PUGACHEV: Sausage! Sausage!

VIKTOR: Art! Art!

ARISTARKH: The Cause! The Cause!

MASHA: Semyon! Semyon!

SERAFIMA: Quiet! Quiet! This is a funeral!

ELPIDI: Yes. Let us pray.

(Everyone kneels, except for EGOR.*)*

MARGARITA: Don't you pray, Egor?

EGOR: It's against my religion.

ARISTARKH: Forgive us, Semyon!

SEMYON: And forgive me, Aristarkh.

SERAFIMA: Ahhhhhhh!

ALL: Help!

SEMYON: *(Climbing out of the coffin)* Food! Food!

MASHA: Semyon!

SEMYON: Margarita! *(Rushes her)*

MARGARITA: *(With a bowl of fruit)* Unhand me, Satan! What do you want?!

SEMYON: Anything! Anything to eat! *(Tears the food out of her hands)* I want to eat! *(Eats)* Except for the one time I snuck out to get a couple of rolls, I've been in there for two days! I want to eat. But more than that, I want to live.

ARISTARKH: What do you mean you want to live?

SEMYON: You tell me what I mean. I'll live anyway you want me to. I'm not picky. Chop off a chicken's head, it runs around without a head—I'll live like that, chop off my head, but let me live. I don't want to die. Not for you, not for them, not for a cause, not to save the world, not for my wife. In life, there was nothing more dear to me than my friends, my family, all the people I love, all the things I love doing, but in the face of death there is nothing that is dear to me, except me. These arms, this leg, this stomach. Comrades, I am in love with my stomach. I am in love with my stomach, comrades!

ELPIDI: What's he talking about?

ARISTARKH: I've never in my life heard such disgusting slobber!

VIKTOR: And I thought he was an artist. *(Exits)*

ARISTARKH: The needs of society must come before the petty needs of one man. That is what society is all about!

SEMYON: Your society is just a factory for slogans! Don't talk to me about society. I'm talking about a man. One man! That man who when he's told that war has been declared, doesn't ask: "War with whom? What are we fighting for?" But instead asks: "How old are they drafting?" That man!—Me!

ARISTARKH: So you're trying to tell me there are no heroes?

SEMYON: I'm trying to tell you what I know. In the circus, there's a bearded lady, so maybe there are heroes too. Anything is possible. But why talk about what's possible, why not talk about what is! And what is—is that there lives in this world one man who is more afraid of death than of anything else.

ARISTARKH: But you're the one who wanted to kill yourself!

ALEXANDER: Isn't that what you told us?

SEMYON: I admit that the thought of suicide brightened my life. My retched inhuman life. But try to understand that here was a man—a man, comrades, and suddenly he's out of work. Why? Was I a troublemaker? Did I run away from our revolution? No! I did not. For a whole month I never left my apartment. I have witnesses. Then why, comrades, am I out of work? So here I stand before you, and I ask this great revolution of ours—revolution, what have you done for me?! I gave you my arm, my right arm, so why do you slap me down? Why was I left out?! I ask, but I hear no answer. So now when our government proclaims—"To All! To All! To All!"—I don't listen, because I know—To All, but not to me. I don't ask much. All the new buildings, all our world stature, all our conquests, I leave them all to you. You can have them. All I ask for myself is a quiet simple life and a decent pay.

ELPIDI: You're his mother-in-law, tell him to shut up.

ALEXANDER: Shut him up!

ARISTARKH: He's preaching a counter-revolution!

SEMYON: God forbid. Has anyone here ever done a single thing against the revolution? We visit each other and bitch about how difficult it is to live. But what's wrong with that? Maybe we need to bitch, in order to keep living! So for God's sake, let's not strip away this our last means for survival, let's not begin to believe what we say. Let's keep moaning that life is difficult, if by saying it's difficult, it makes life easier. Even if we have to whisper: "It's a hard life." Then let's whisper. Comrades, I ask you in the name of millions of Russians, let us whisper. No one will hear us anyway what with all the construction going on.

PUGACHEV: What's going on here? I don't believe this. Up to now I've kept my mouth shut, but I don't think I can anymore. You... You crook! You coward! You scum!

You think you can just dig our grave and then crawl away. You've destroyed me, I will see that you're shot!

RAISA: Shoot him!

VOICES: Shoot him! Shoot him!

SEMYON: Masha! Mama! What are they saying?! They can't mean it! Shoot me—why? What have I done? All the money you've spent I'll pay back. Every last kopeck, I'll pay back. Somehow. I'll sell my bureau, if I have to. I'll stop eating. I'll make Masha do your laundry. I'll send my mother-in-law to the mines. I'll become a beggar. I'll beg. I'm begging: let me live! *(Falls to his knees)*

ARISTARKH: Pathetic. *(Spits)*

SEMYON: Who did that? Who went *(Spits)*? Whoever went *(Spits)* I want him to come here and take this. *(Takes out the revolver)* Take this revolver, come here, come here!

ARISTARKH: Stop with the jokes. Put your pistol away. Put it away!

SEMYON: Scared? Are you scared? Then why have you been accusing me?! What is my crime?! That I'm still alive? So I live, but I don't bother anybody. I've never harmed anyone in my whole life. I've never hurt a fly. If I am to blame for anyone's death, let them speak now!!!!

(VIKTOR runs in.)

VIKTOR: Fedia Pitunin has shot himself. *(Pause)* He left a note.

ARISTARKH: What does it say?

VIKTOR: "Podsekalnikov is right. Why bother."

(Curtain)

END OF PLAY